Cambridge Latin C

Book III

Student Study Book

FOURTH EDITION

CAMBRIDGE
UNIVERSITY PRESS

CAMBRIDGE UNIVERSITY PRESS

Cambridge, New York, Melbourne, Madrid, Cape Town, Singapore, São Paulo

Cambridge University Press
The Edinburgh Building, Cambridge CB2 8RU, UK

www.cambridge.org
Information on this title: www.cambridge.org/9780521685955

First published by the University of Cambridge School Classics Project
as *Independent Learning Manual Book III* 2004
Fourth edition 2007

Printed in the United Kingdom at the University Press, Cambridge

A catalogue record for this publication is available from the British Library

ISBN   978-0-521-68595-5 paperback

Preface

This *Student Study Book* is designed to be used in conjunction with Book III of the *Cambridge Latin Course* (ISBN 978-0-521-79794-8). It is intended for use by students in the following situations:

- students learning Latin on their own
- students on short courses who have to do much of the work on their own
- students being taught privately and requiring additional support material
- students who are catching up after illness or a change of schools
- students working ahead of the rest of the group
- teachers who wish to set cover work for a class
- classes in which independent learning is encouraged
- classes containing groups of students working at different levels.

An *Answer Key* is also available (ISBN 978-0-521-68596-2), as are online resources and e-tutor support (see page iv).

The *Student Study Books* are re-workings of the earlier *Independent Learning Manuals*. In the creation of the original materials we benefited greatly from the advice and help of many teachers and students. In particular we should like to thank the following: Julien Melville for generously allowing us to make use of his own materials; Richard Woff, Neil Williams, Eileen Emmett, Betty Munday, Alex Nightingale and Wilf O'Neill for reading the draft materials and making many helpful suggestions and criticisms; Helen Vicat, whose ideas for pictures and skill in executing them have enlivened several pages; Helen Forte for her talented and witty artwork; Jean Groombridge; Christine Spillane; Joan Wootten; Jill Dalladay, for her suggestions for comprehension questions and exercises; Roger Dalladay, for his notes on the illustrations; Christine Simister, who pioneered the use of independent learning materials with the *Cambridge Latin Course*.

We are grateful to the following teachers and students who trialled the materials: Lucy Harrow and students at St Teresa's School, Dorking; Neil Williams' students at South Park Sixth Form College, Middlesbrough; David Karsten and students at Ranelagh School, Bracknell; Marian Small and students at St Margaret's School, Bushey; Jean Hubbard and her students at Banbury Community Education Council and Pat Story and her students at Coleridge Community College, Cambridge.

Finally, we should like to thank Betty Munday and Margaret Widdess for much detailed and demanding work; Debbie James for her meticulous reading of the texts; Maire Collins for designing and setting the original texts with such patience, care and ingenuity; and Jean Hubbard and Pat Story for all their work in developing, creating and editing the original *Independent Learning Manuals*. To these and all our other helpers we are much indebted.

Cambridge School Classics Project
July 2006

Introduction

Welcome to *Cambridge Latin Course Book III* which is set in Roman Bath and Chester.

What you need to begin

The *Cambridge Latin Course Book III*, Fourth Edition.

If you are working on your own without a teacher to mark your work, you will need the *Student Study Book III: Answer Key*.

These books are obtainable from Cambridge University Press.

Online resources

All the stories in *Cambridge Latin Course Book III* are available online in 'exploring' format. This allows you to click any word and see the vocabulary definition for that word instantly. You will also find interactive comprehensions, activities for practising grammar and many carefully selected weblinks for each Stage of the Book. All the resources are available at www.CambridgeSCP.com.

E-tutor support

If you would like tutored support through the Book, we can provide you with a distance e-tutor and study guide. You may begin your course whenever you choose and study at whatever pace suits you – your tutor will be on hand to help you for up to 40 weeks. All you need is a computer with an internet connection and an email account. For more information, please visit www.CambridgeSCP.com.

How to use this Student Study Book

If you turn to p. 1, you will find instructions for working through Stage 21. The Book has the same headings as those in the textbook and gives page references, e.g. **Model sentences** pp. 2–4. Start working through the material in the order given in this Book, which is sometimes different from that in the textbook. This is to give you more variety.

How to check your answers

Check

This sign tells you when to check your answers.

You do this by using the separate *Answer Key* if you do not have a teacher to help you.

When you are checking your translations, you may find that you have used different words from those in the *Answer Key*. If their *meaning* is the same, your translation will be correct. In order to help you, the *Answer Key* often gives a rather literal translation and you may be able to think of better, more idiomatic expressions.

How to learn efficiently

It is better to have several short sessions a week than one or two long ones. Try to find short periods of time (even 10 minutes) to revise what you have learnt. This is particularly important when learning vocabulary or grammar.

Use active learning methods whenever possible; for example, in learning vocabulary, learn a few words and their meanings; then cover up the English meanings and give yourself a mini-test; better still, ask someone to test you. Then learn the next batch and give yourself another test.

How to keep track of your progress

You will find a **Progress record** at the end of each Stage in this Book. You can use it to record work as you do it or to note any questions you would like to ask your teacher or e-tutor. Use the Revision section for any particular points from the whole Stage that you need to continue to revise.

How to pronounce Latin

The best way to learn to pronounce Latin is to listen to your teacher reading from the textbook and then imitate him or her.

Both in the textbook and in this Book you will see that many Latin words have marks over some of the vowels. This is to help you to remember that those vowels have a long sound; e.g. ā in **māter** is pronounced like the *a* in *father*.

There is a **Short guide to the pronunciation of Latin** on p. 108. Further help can be found online at www.CambridgeSCP.com in the 'Links' section of the Teachers' Area of the *Cambridge Latin Course*.

Stage 21 Aquae Sūlis

In Book II Quintus told Cogidubnus
about his eventful stay in Alexandria.
In Book III the focus is once again on
Roman Britain. We move from the
palace at Fishbourne to Roman Bath,
Aquae Sulis, which was famous for its
hot springs and baths, as it still is today.
Aquae Sulis means 'The waters of Sulis'.
Sulis was a Celtic goddess.

Picture p. 1

This is an enlarged photograph of part of a saucepan handle. It shows a worshipper
making an offering outside a temple at a covered altar, rather like a lararium.
The saucepan is a special one: it is made of silver and parts of it are gilded, as
you can see in the photograph. Its connection with Bath will be explained later
in the Stage.

Model sentences pp. 2–4

Study the pictures and sentences and then answer the questions below. New and
unfamiliar words are in the boxes.

Sentences 1

oppidō: oppidum	*town*
fabrī: faber	*craftsman, workman*
thermās: thermae	*baths*
exstruēbant: exstruere	*build*
architectus	*architect, builder*

a What were the craftsmen building in Bath?

b What was the architect doing?

c How can we tell from the picture that he was a Roman citizen?

Sentences 2

perītus	*skilful*
ab architectō	*by the architect*

a What was the first craftsman doing?

b Why did the architect praise him?

c Fill in the missing word in this translation:

The craftsman, having been _____ by the architect, was very happy.

Sentences 3

fontem: fōns	*spring, fountain*
graviter ferēbat: graviter ferre	*take badly*

a What was the second craftsman doing?

b Why did the architect urge him on?

c Fill in the missing two words in this translation:

The craftsman, _____ _____ urged on by the architect, took the criticism (**rem**) *badly.*

Clue: see **Sentence 2c** above.

d Why did he not reply?

Sentences 4

balneum	*bath*
īnsolenter	*insolently, rudely*

a What was the third workman doing?

b How did the architect react to him? Why?

c Complete this sentence: *The workman, _____ _____ _____ by the architect, replied insolently.*

Sentences 5

a When did the architect summon his slaves?

b What did the slaves do to the workman?

c Which phrase in the second sentence tells you that these slaves were the same as the slaves mentioned in the first sentence? Translate the phrase.

Sentences 6

linguam: lingua	*tongue*
melius est	*it would be better*

a Why did the architect want the workman to drink the sacred water?

b Which Latin word describes the architect? What does it mean?

Check

fōns sacer p. 5

Read lines 1–10 and answer the questions.

1 Where did Quintus spend the winter?

2 Where did he often go?

3 What did he do there? Why?

4 When did Cogidubnus fall seriously ill?

5 Complete this translation of the sentence **multī medicī ... quaesīvērunt** (lines 6–7).

Many doctors, <u>sent</u> _____ <u>for</u> _____ <u>came</u> *to the palace, sought a cure for the illness.*

6 Translate the sentence that shows the doctors were unsuccessful.

7 Why did the king ask Quintus for his advice (lines 9–10)? *tu es vir sapiens*

8 What question did he ask Quintus? *ad fontem sacrum ire debeo?*

Now read the rest of the story.

9 Why did Cogidubnus think the water of the sacred spring might help him?

10 What two new buildings had appeared in Bath (lines 14–16)? *baths + Sulis temple*

11 The following phrases show that Cogidubnus was responsible for these buildings. Can you translate them?

a architectus Rōmānus, ā mē missus (line 14). *a Roman architect sent by me*

b templum deae Sūlis, ā meīs fabrīs aedificātum (lines 15–16). *a temple to goddess Sulis built by my workmen*

12 **ego deam saepe honōrāvī** (line 16). What did he hope for in return? *fortasse dea me sanare potest*

13 How does Cogidubnus describe Salvius (line 17)? *f. magnae sapientiae*

14 What does Salvius think Cogidubnus ought to do (lines 19–20)? *tibi testamentum facere*

15

Look at this drawing and write in the balloons what you think each person is thinking or feeling.

Check

Lūcius Marcius Memor pp. 6–7

Read lines 1–20 and answer questions 1–6. The questions will often give you clues about the meaning of the Latin, and the marks are a guide to the number of points required in your answers.

Check

Further work You may prefer to finish the story and the questions before you do this further work.

Give the meanings and descriptions of the words in the table. There are two superlatives, two infinitives, two imperatives and one present participle. The first one is done for you.

Line	Latin	English	Description
1	maximae	very large	superlative
2	nōtissimus	*very famous*	*"*
5	excitāre	*to excite*	*infinit*
7	dormiēns	*sleeping*	*p p*
9	surge	*get up*	*imp*
11	abī	*go away*	*imp*
12	surgere	*to get up*	*infin*

Check

Read the rest of the story and answer questions 7–12.

Check

Further work Translate the following descriptions of people. To whom do they refer?

Line	Description	Translation	Person(s)
21–2	quam fessus sum!	*how tired I am*	*Memor*
25	paucī (twice)	*few men*	*Men in Br*
30	territus	*terrified*	*Cephalus*
31	vehementer clāmantēs	*shouting loudly*	*Very many men*

General question What impression have you gained from this story of the characters of Memor and Cephalus? *lazy, drunk ... must look at job*

Check

Aquae Sulis and its baths pp. 14–20

Read this section and study the pictures. Then answer the following questions.

1 Where is Bath (paragraph 1)? If you are unsure, find it on the map, p. 139.

2 Choose one of the following questions. When you check your answer, also read the suggested answer to the question you did not choose.

    a Imagine that you are Rusonia Aventina or Julius Vitalis (see the last paragraph on p. 14). Describe your visit to the baths and temple. What would you do and feel?

Or

    b If you had been a Celt living in the area, what would you have felt about the building of the baths and temple and the development of Bath as a tourist centre?

3 Look at the pictures of the temple, p. 18. For a close-up of the circular decoration in the middle of the pediment see the photograph and caption, p. 40, and the cover of the book.

4 Read again the last two paragraphs on p. 18. Study the photograph on p. 19, and then the drawing above with descriptions of the finds from the sacred spring. Some objects have no descriptions. Can you identify them?

    a _____ (three objects).

    b Pewter dish.

    c Silver saucepan. The handle shown on p. 1 was attached to a saucepan like this.

    d Bronze saucepan. The decoration was originally filled with enamel.

    e _____ (two objects).

    f Bone handle of clasp knife.

    g Curse tablet. This will be explained in the next Stage.

    h Bronze washer from small military catapult, similar in strength to medieval crossbow.

    i Ivory carving of a pair of breasts, perhaps given to the goddess in gratitude for healing.

j   See close-up, p. 20. _____.

k   Sheet of bronze with cut-out pattern, perhaps part of priest's ritual dress.

l   _____.

m   _____ (three objects).

n   Tin mask, 33 cm high, previously attached to wooden backing, used in the temple ritual.

o   See small objects at the bottom of p. 19 and paragraph 2, p. 18.

   _____.

p   Pewter inkpot.

Check

senātor advenit p. 8

Translate this cartoon version of the story. You will need to use the vocabulary on p. 8.

1   Cephalus ā thermīs rediit. cubiculum rūrsus intrāvit Memoremque dormientem excitāvit.

cūr prohibēs mē dormīre? stultior es quam asinus.

aliquid novī nūntiāre volō. senātōrem thermīs appropinquantem cōnspexī.

2

quis est ille senātor? unde vēnit? senātōrem vidēre nōlō.

melius est tibi hunc senātōrem vidēre. nam Gāius Salvius est.

num Gāius Salvius Līberālis? nōn crēdō tibi.

3   Cephalus tamen facile eī persuāsit, quod Salvius iam in āream thermārum equitābat.

fer mihi togam! fer calceōs! ōrnāmenta mea ubi sunt? vocā servōs! quam īnfēlīx sum! Salvius hūc venit, vir summae auctōritātis, quem colere maximē volō.

4   Memor celerrimē togam calceōsque induit. Cephalus eī ōrnāmenta trādidit, ex armāriō raptim extracta.

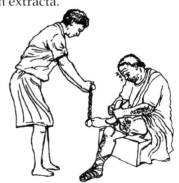

haruspex lībertum innocentem vituperābat, lībertus Salvium.

Before you check your translation, answer these questions.

1 There are five different questions in the balloons. Can you spot them and say what they mean?

2 Memor says to Cephalus 'stultior es quam asinus'. *as*

Memor says of himself 'quam īnfēlīx sum!' *how*

What does quam mean in each of these sentences?

3 What do the words in **bold type** mean in these sentences? Which noun do they agree with? *by*

a Cephalus Memorem **dormientem** excitāvit.

b senātōrem thermīs **appropinquantem** cōnspexī.

Check

Picture p. 8

The inscription on this statue base is the only evidence we have of Memor's existence. All the stories about him are made up.

To the goddess Sulis

L(ucius) Marcius Memor

Harusp(ex)

D(ono) D(edit) – gave (this statue) as a gift

You will see that the carver has sometimes run two or three letters together, for example, A and E in DEAE. Can you copy the way in which he has compressed Memor's full name?

In the third line it looks as if the original lettering was HAR, placed dead centre, and that VSP was added later to make the abbreviation understandable to the Britons.

Memor's job as haruspex was to examine the entrails of animals when they had been sacrificed. Depending on their appearance, he would announce whether the gods approved or disapproved of what the sacrificer wanted.

Although Memor was less important than Salvius, he belonged, as a haruspex, to a wealthy class and could afford to set up a statue of Sulis Minerva. The statue would demonstrate to all who visited the temple his generosity and piety.

The statue base still stands near the altar in front of the temple in the position in which it was excavated in 1965.

About the language: perfect passive participles pp. 9–10

Paras 1–3   Read and then answer these questions.

1 In paragraph 1 why are the endings of **quaerentēs** and **sedentem** different?

2 In paragraph 2 which noun does **aedificātae** describe?

Para. 4   Do the exercise as instructed, using the table below for the second part of the exercise.

Perfect passive participle	Noun	Singular or plural
a		
b		
c		
d		
e		
f		

Para. 5   Study the different ways of translating the participles.

Further exercise   Translate these sentences, first literally and then in more natural English.

1 faber, ab architectō vituperātus, īnsolenter respondit.

2 multī medicī, ad aulam arcessītī, remedium morbī quaesīvērunt.

3 Memor, ā lībertō tandem excitātus, ūnum oculum aperuit.

4 Cephalus, ā dominō īrātō territus, invītus exiit.

5 aderant mīlitēs, ab hostibus vulnerātī.

> You may find it helpful for the future to learn an example and its translation by heart, e.g. **faber ab architectō laudātus** *the craftsman, having been praised by the architect.*

Check

Memor rem suscipit I pp. 10–11

Memor has now pulled himself together to meet his distinguished visitor. Salvius has a proposition to put to Memor.

The part of Salvius has been translated for you below. Translate the words of Memor to complete the scene.

Salvius and Memor, walking alone in the garden, are having a serious conversation.

Salvius: *Lucius Marcius Memor, you are a man of the highest intelligence. I want you to undertake an important task.*

Memor: _____

_____

_____

Salvius: Tiberius Claudius Cogidubnus, king of the Regnenses, has recently arrived here. Cogidubnus, who has fallen seriously ill (lit. *has fallen into a serious illness*), wants to drink the water from the sacred spring.

Memor: _____
_____
_____

Salvius: I don't want you to make Cogidubnus well. I want you to do the opposite.

Memor: _____
_____

Salvius: Yes! What's more, although you are so busy, I want you to carry out this job yourself.

Memor: _____
_____
_____

Salvius: You are a very shrewd man (lit. *a man of the greatest shrewdness*). You can carry out this mission. Not only I, but also the emperor, wants this. For Cogidubnus has often annoyed the Romans. The emperor trusts me, not Cogidubnus. The emperor promises you an appropriate reward. Surely you don't want to refuse the reward promised by the emperor?

Memor: _____

Salvius: I don't know. I say only this to you: the emperor awaits the death of Cogidubnus.

Memor: _____
_____

Salvius: Life, my dear Memor, is full of difficult things.
(Salvius goes out.)

Check

Now answer the following questions:

1 **in hortō sōlī ambulantēs** (line 1). Why are Salvius and Memor doing this?
2 Why do you think Salvius calls Memor **vir summae prūdentiae** (line 3)?
3 **tālem rem ... sum** (line 5). How much of this do you think is true?
4 **exspectant ... et fabrī** (lines 6–7). Why does Memor include these details?
5 Read Memor's speech (lines 5–7) aloud. Where does your tone change? Why?
6 **Cogidubnus, quī ... bibere vult** (lines 9–10). What does Memor think Salvius is asking him to do? How do you know?

7 When Memor understands Salvius' plan, why is he reluctant to carry it out?

8 **Cogidubnus ... Rōmānōs saepe vexāvit** (line 24). Is Salvius' statement true? Give a reason.

9 Why does Memor finally agree to carry out Salvius' plan?

10 Read lines 28 to the end again. How does Salvius respond to Memor's plea for help?

Check

Further work   In this story there are several examples of the irregular verbs **volō**, **nōlō**, **sum** and **possum**. Turn to p. 158 and revise the present and imperfect forms of these verbs. **nōlō** is not given because it follows the same pattern as **volō**.

Translate the following sentences and then turn the verbs in **bold type** into the imperfect tense and give the new meaning.

1 **volō** tē rem magnam suscipere.

2 quid **vīs** mē facere?

3 hoc facere **nōlō**.

4 Cogidubnus **est** vir clārissimus.

5 rēgem interficere nōn **possum**.

6 nōnne imperātōrem adiuvāre **possumus**?

Check

Memor rem suscipit II p. 11

Translate this scene in your head.

Check

Now answer the following questions.

1 How and when do the moods of each character change during the scene? How would Memor say his final line?

2 Revise the dative case by translating these pairs of sentences. The first sentence of each pair is taken from the story, the second is new, but related to the first. Highlight or underline the dative cases in the Latin sentences and in the translations.

a cūr mihi vīnum offers?

lībertus dominō vīnum offert.

b cōnsilium, quod mihi prōpōnis, perīculōsum est.

Cephalus haruspicī cōnsilium callidum prōpōnit.

c nūllīs servīs cōnfīdō.

Memor lībertō cōnfīdit.

d iubeō tē ipsum Cogidubnō pōculum praebēre.

necesse est Cephalō venēnum rēgī dare.

Check

If you have got more than two datives wrong, revise the forms and meanings by studying the noun tables on pp. 146–7. For **mihi** see p. 152.

3   The perfect passive participles in the box below occur in this scene. Write down the Latin nouns they describe and translate the sentences into natural English.

One participle is not in a sentence.

Line	Perfect passive participle	Latin noun described	Translated sentence
1	vocātus		
6	vexātus		
10	datum		
11	cēlātum		
17	dēlectātus		

Check

Word patterns: adjectives and adverbs p. 12

Word patterns is a new section which you will find in every Stage in this Book. It shows you how words are linked together or built up from one another. For example, in paragraph 1 you will see how an adjective, **laetus** *happy*, can be changed to mean *happily* by making its ending **-ē** instead of **-us**. Understanding patterns like these will help you to read Latin more accurately.

Study paragraphs 1 and 2 and work through paragraphs 3–5 as instructed. Some of the words are new, but use the pattern you have studied in paragraph 1 to help you.

Check

Practising the language p. 13

Ex. 1   This exercise revises the nominative, accusative and genitive, singular and plural of nouns. After completing and translating each sentence, write down the case and number of the noun you have chosen.

Check

If you have made more than two wrong choices, revise the case endings of nouns on pp. 146–7 before going on to Exercise 2.

Ex. 2   This is a new kind of exercise. Study the instructions and example carefully before you start. Think which form of the noun and verb is needed before selecting from the pairs of words. Write out your Latin sentence, keeping to the same Latin word order.

Ex. 3   This exercise practises all the tenses of the verb you have learnt so far: present, imperfect, perfect and pluperfect, and the first three persons singular: I, you, s/he.

Be careful with sentence **e**, because the verb is irregular.

Check

If you have had problems with this exercise, be sure to complete the **Revision** section on the next page.

Vocabulary p. 168

Read paragraphs 2 and 3 on p. 168. These explain how the verbs in the following Vocabulary and the checklists are listed in Book III. Work through the examples in paragraph 4. If you have problems refer again to paragraph 2 to help you.

Check

Vocabulary checklist 21 p. 20

Learn the checklist, including all parts of the verbs. Then answer these questions. Use an English dictionary to help you if necessary.

1   In each regiment the commanding officer has an *adjutant*. What is his job?

2   Why are some plants described as *annuals* and others as *perennials*?

3   Think of two English words beginning with *circum*.

4   What is an *efficient* person?

5   The judge said he regarded the crime with the utmost *gravity*. What did he mean? Can you think of another meaning of the word?

6   What would it mean if someone took a *morbid* interest in hospital TV programmes?

7   What do you often call this sign '+' in mathematics?

8   What is the connection between **pretium** and **pretiōsus**?

9   Who is referred to as **homō sapiēns**?

10   Which checklist words are to be found within the following English words: *conceal*, *endure*, *replenish*? What do the English words mean?

Check

Language test

1   Translate the following sentences.

   a   fabrī, ā rēge missī, thermās templumque aedificāvērunt.

   b   thermae, ā fabrīs aedificātae, erant maximae.

   c   Cephalus, ā Memore iussus, vīnum intulit.

   d   faber, in balneum dēiectus, architectum vituperāvit.

   e   Salvius, ā Cogidubnō rogātus, cōnsilium dedit.

   f   Memor praemium ab Imperātōre prōmissum recūsāre nōlēbat.

In each sentence pick out the noun and participle pair and state whether it is singular or plural.

2 Translate the following sentences and give the case and number of the nouns in **bold type**.

For example:

templum **deae** prope thermās stābat.

The temple of the goddess stood near the baths.

deae: genitive singular.

a Quīntus **rēgī** multa dē urbe Alexandrīae nārrābat.

b Memor, quī iam multās hōrās dormīverat, ūnum **oculum** aperuit.

c Memorem exspectābant multī fabrī, nōnnūllī **mercātōrēs**.

d Cephalus **servīs** mandāta dominī saepe dabat.

e Memor verbīs **lībertī** nōn crēdidit.

f 'ēheu!' inquit Memor. 'hoc oppidum est plēnum **hominum** molestissimōrum.'

Revision

Verbs

1 The following endings all denote persons of the verb. Can you identify them? The first one is done for you.

-nt	they
-ō	
-mus	
-tis	
-istis	
-t	
-m	
-istī	
-ī	
-s	

2 The following verbs are in the Vocabulary checklist for this Stage. What does each of these forms mean?

a adiuvō; adiūvī; adiūvistī.

b cēlant; cēlāmus; cēlāvimus.

c efficitis; effēcistis; effēcerātis.

d iubēbās; iussistī; iusseram.

Adjectives pp. 148–9

Para. 1 Study the table and compare the forms of **bonus** with those of the first and second declension nouns on p. 146.

Para. 2 Study the forms of **fortis** and **ingēns**. Note especially the nominative singular forms. Then compare all their other cases with the nouns of the third declension on p. 147.

Paras 3 and 4 Write out as instructed.

Further work In the checklists and in the **Vocabulary** at the end of the Book adjectives like **bonus** and **fortis** are listed with their nominative singular forms. Those like **ingēns** are listed with nominative and genitive singular. Arrange these adjectives in the correct columns below, writing them out in the same form as the headings:

attonitus   sapiēns   trīstis   furēns   dulcis   stultus

bonus, bona, bonum	fortis, forte	ingēns, *gen.* ingentis

Check

Progress record

Stage 21 Aquae Sūlis	Done	Revised	Any problems?
Model sentences			
fōns sacer			
Lūcius Marcius Memor			
Aquae Sulis and its baths			
senātor advenit			
About the language: perfect passive participles			
Memor rem suscipit I			
Memor rem suscipit II			
Word patterns: adjectives and adverbs			
Practising the language			
Vocabulary			
Vocabulary checklist 21			
Language test			
Revision			

Stage 22 dēfīxiō

In Stage 21 the stories were about people connected with the baths, such as the manager, Memor, and his freedman, Cephalus.

In this Stage we meet some of the ordinary inhabitants of Aquae Sulis and two Roman soldiers who are on leave in the town.

Picture p. 21

This is one of the small sheets of pewter or lead, called a **dēfīxiō**, which was found in the sacred spring (see p. 18). It has an inscription which at first sight makes no sense. In this Stage you will learn about this defixio and be able to read its message.

Model sentences pp. 22–3

Read the sentences and answer the questions.

ingressus	*having entered*
cōnspicātus	*having caught sight of*
precātus	*having prayed to*
regressus	*having returned*
adeptus	*having obtained*

Sentences 1 Which part of the baths did the thief hurry to? What had he done before this? What do you think was his intention? Clue: What is he carrying?

Sentences 2 a Translate the first sentence.

 b Where did the thief hide? Which Latin words give you the reason why he did this?

Sentences 3 a What was the old man doing when he advanced to the fountain?

 b Fill in the missing words.

 The old man _____ to heaven and _____

 _____ from the goddess Sulis.

Sentence 4 **senex … amulētum in fontem iniēcit.** When did the old man do this? Why do you think he did it?

Sentences 5 a What prompted the thief to return to the spring?

      b Translate the second sentence.

Sentences 6 a Which Latin words in the first sentence tell you that the thief retrieved the amulet?

      b Why was he astonished by what he read?

      c Give a reason why he had cause to regret his visit to the baths.

Check

Vilbia p. 24

This story takes place in a pub run by Latro, who does not have an easy life. One of his daughters, Vilbia, has fallen madly in love with Modestus, a Roman soldier.
    Read lines 1–10 and answer the questions in your head.

1 What is the relationship between Vilbia and Rubria?

2 What kind of man is Latro?

3 **multa sunt pōcula sordida** (line 5). Give a reason for this situation.

4 **Vilbia … patrī nōn pāruit** (line 8). What does this mean? What further proof of this do we have in this paragraph?

Further work From lines 1–6 write down:

1 one present participle

2 two nouns in the genitive case

3 one imperative (order)

4 one comparative adjective.

Check

Student groups Half of you could read the following conversation between Vilbia and Rubria (lines 11–31) and half read the next story, **Modestus** p. 25. In each case write down the answers to the appropriate questions. You could then exchange answers and mark each other's work. In this way you will get to read both stories.

Individual students Finish reading **Vilbia** and answer the following questions.

Then read the translation of **Modestus** in the *Answer Key* alongside the Latin text and answer only questions 9 and 10 on that story.

Questions lines 11–31

1   What impresses Rubria about the brooch?

2   How did Vilbia get the brooch?

3   What is Rubria's opinion of Roman soldiers in general (lines 16–17)?

4   **est vir maximae virtūtis** (line 18). What examples of Modestus' courage does Vilbia give?

5   Does Rubria believe her sister (lines 20–1)? Give reasons for your answer.

6   How did Vilbia meet Modestus (lines 23–4)?

7   Why was she attracted to him?

8   Who is Bulbus? Why does Rubria warn her sister about him?

9   Why does Vilbia prefer Modestus to Bulbus (lines 28–31)?

10   How far do you agree with the following descriptions of Vilbia?

  naive   shallow   unfaithful   foolish

  In each case give a reason for your answer.

 Check

Modestus p. 25

We now meet Modestus and his friend, Strythio, on their way to Latro's pub. For directions about reading this story, see **Vilbia** above.

1   What does line 3 show about Modestus' attitude to Strythio?

2   Why does Strythio consider himself lucky (lines 4–6)?

3   What example of his courage does Modestus give (line 7)?

4   **tam fortis et pulcher es** (lines 8–9). What effect has this had on Vilbia?

5   **fībulam** (line 13). How had Modestus got this brooch?

6   How did Vilbia respond to this present (lines 16–18)?

7   What do lines 19–20 show about Modestus?

8   What ends the friends' conversation?

9   In this scene Modestus is compared to Mars and Hercules. Why would he be pleased with these comparisons?

10   **Strȳthiō ... eum dērīdet** (lines 1–2). Look through Strythio's speeches again. Pick out two examples where you think Strythio is making fun of Modestus and explain each of your choices.

Check

About the language 1: perfect active participles p. 26

Paras 1–2   Read. There is a difference in the translation of the participles in the two paragraphs. What is it?

Look at the pictures and then translate the captions, highlighting or underlining the perfect participles. Which one is the perfect active participle?

a   b

amulētum, in aquam coniectum,   fūr, ad fontem regressus, amulētum
erat aureum.   in aquā invēnit.

Para. 3   Translate the sentences and complete the exercise as instructed. Enter the participles and nouns in the table below.

	Participle	Noun	Number
a			
b			
c			
d			
e			

Check

Para. 4   There are only a small number of perfect active participles. Although their endings look the same as perfect passive participles, you will usually be able to translate each kind correctly because of the general sense of the sentence.

a   puellae, ā patre vituperātae, nōn respondērunt.

The girls, having been blamed by their father, did not reply.

vituperātae must mean *having been blamed* because of the phrase **ā patre** *by their father*. *Having blamed* would not make sense.

b   Vilbia, culīnam ingressa, sorōrī fībulam ostendit.

Vilbia, having entered the kitchen, showed the brooch to her sister.

ingressa must mean *having entered* because it has an accusative, **culīnam** *kitchen*, and no other translation would make sense.

The most common perfect active participles are given in the Stage checklists. It would be a good idea to write down a separate list of these and add to it as you go through the Book.

amor omnia vincit pp. 27–30

scaena prīma p. 27

In this scene we are back in Latro's pub, shortly before Modestus and Strythio arrive.

Read lines 1–2. Gutta's part is translated for you. Read it with the Latin and translate the part of Bulbus in the spaces left below.

Gutta: (friend of Bulbus) *How unlucky you are! Not only have you lost your girl, but also your money.*

Bulbus: _____

_____

Gutta: *How can you hold on to her? A Roman soldier, a man of outstanding bravery, is after her. Hey! I've thrown a Venus! Innkeeper! I order you to bring more wine.*

Bulbus: _____

_____

_____

_____

_____

_____

Gutta: *It's not safe for girls to go through the streets of this town. Such (so great) is the cheek of these soldiers. Good heavens! You are even more unlucky. You've thrown a dog again. You owe me another denarius.*

Bulbus: _____

_____

_____

_____

_____

(Enter Modestus and Strythio, whom Bulbus does not see.)

_____

_____

Gutta: *Good heavens! You are very unlucky. Look! Modestus himself is coming towards us. I must leave as quickly as possible.*
(Exit, running.)

Check

Now answer these questions:

1 **mīles Rōmānus** (line 7). What is his name? How does Gutta's description of him seem to contradict what he says later about Roman soldiers (lines 15–16)? Can you explain this?

2 Write down the two Latin sentences which refer to these pictures.

a

Latin sentence: _____

b

Latin sentence: _____

How would you translate these sentences in modern English?

3 As things go from bad to worse for Bulbus, he is described as **īnfēlīx**, then **īnfēlīcior** and finally **īnfēlīcissimus**. What do these words mean?

4 **intrant ... exīre** (lines 23–8). Read these lines again. What makes Gutta say that Bulbus is **īnfēlīcissimus**?

Check

scaena secunda p. 28

Bulbus and Modestus now confront one another.

1 **tū ... in magnō perīculō es** (lines 3–4). Modestus implies that he is ready to use force against Bulbus. How does he actually put this into practice?

2 Lines 6–8 contain the words describing how each character played his part in the fight. Match each word to the character it refers to.

Description	Character
invītus	
fortiter	
ferōciter	

3 Which character do you think is

a the bravest?

b the most cowardly?

Refer to the text and give your reasons.

4 To what extent does Vilbia's behaviour in this scene agree or disagree with your previous opinion of her?

5 **magnam partem huius colloquiī audīvit** (line 29).

a Why has Bulbus not heard the whole of the conversation? *Clue:* Think what happened to him in the fight.

b What points will Bulbus have especially noted from the conversation?

Check

Picture p. 29

This photograph of the sacred spring is taken from above the windows which are shown in the model sentences and which survive today. All the buildings you see here are much later in date.

scaena tertia pp. 29–30

Bulbus has now thought of a plan to take vengeance on Modestus.
Write out a translation of lines 1–13.
Read the rest of the story and then answer the questions.

1 From the stage direction (lines 14–15) describe what Gutta and Modestus are doing.

2 **quam rauca est vōx tua!** (line 19). What reason does Modestus suggest for this?

3 When does he realise that something peculiar has happened to Vilbia?

4 In line 16 Modestus describes himself as **fortissimus mīlitum**. What does this mean? Is it shown to be true by his behaviour in lines 27–31?

5 When the real Vilbia comes in, she is **perterrita** (line 26), but by line 32 she has become **īrāta**. What has caused the change?

6 **victōribus decōrum est victīs parcere** (line 36). Who spoke these words before in **scaena secunda**? Why do you think Bulbus repeats them? What effect would they have on Vilbia?

7 Who do you consider to be the 'winners' and who the 'losers' in this play? Why?

Check

About the language 2: more about the genitive p. 31

Paras 1–2 Read.

Para. 3 Translate the examples in your head.

Further work Complete the examples by filling in the genitive singular case of the noun in brackets and then translate them. Use the **Vocabulary** section on pp. 170–84 to help you.

Latin phrase	Translation
nimium .... (clāmor)	
plūs .... (cibus)	
nihil .... (ars)	
aliquid .... (praemium)	
multum .... (negōtium)	

If you are learning French, you have probably met similar phrases.

Latin	French
satis pecūniae	assez d'argent
nimium vīnī	trop de vin
multum aquae	beaucoup d'eau

Paras 4–5 Read and translate the further examples.

Further work Replace the word in **bold type** in these examples with one of the genitive phrases in paragraphs 4 and 5 which has a similar meaning.

1 mīles **fortissimus**   4 ancilla **doctissima**

2 uxor **optima**   5 **hoc** cōnsilium

3 fūr **scelestus**   6 faber **stultissimus**

Check

Magic and curses pp. 34–5

Read the information and study the pictures of tablets. The Vilbia curse can be seen more clearly in the enlarged version on p. 21.

1 In **amor omnia vincit** (p. 27) Bulbus tells Gutta that he has put a curse on Modestus. In your opinion, did this have an influence on what subsequently happened to Modestus? Support your answer from events in the story.

2 Draw a square to represent a curse tablet. Using the information on pp. 34–5, design an inscription in English for the tablet, outlining the crime and intended punishment of an imaginary enemy. You could write it backwards and then get a friend to decipher it.

Describe what you would do with the inscribed tablet.

Check

Word patterns: more adjectives and adverbs p. 32

Paras 1–2 Read.

Para. 3 Work out the answers in your head.

Paras 4–5 Write out the answers.

Further work 1 Read the following sentences and fill in the gaps.

a The adjectives in paragraph 1 belong to the 1st and 2nd declensions. Their adverbs end in ___.

b The adjectives in paragraphs 2 and 3 belong to the 3rd declension. Their adverbs end in __.

2 What would be the adverbs from these adjectives? If in doubt, study the examples in paragraphs 1–3. Give the meanings of both the adjectives and adverbs.

benignus   gravis   crūdēlis   malus   pessimus   ēlegāns

Check

Practising the language p. 33

Ex. 1 First work out the meaning of the sentence before choosing the noun in brackets that makes good sense. You will find that the choice is between the genitive and dative form of the noun. Check, if necessary, with the tables on pp. 146–7. Translate the sentences.

Ex. 2 First work out the meaning of the sentence and think of the case and number of the noun which the adjective describes. Then choose the right adjective to fill in the gap. If necessary, revise the forms of adjectives on p. 148. Translate the sentences.

Check

Vocabulary checklist 22 p. 36

In this checklist, as in **Vocabulary checklist 21**, the verb forms include the perfect passive participle. Also listed are some of the perfect active participles met in this Stage.

> You will find it helpful to start making a list of these perfect active participles and to add to it as you meet more of them in later checklists.

After learning the checklist, answer the questions.

1 In art, figures of Cupids are sometimes called *amoretti*. What is the connection?

2 Someone you know is described as *eligible* for promotion. Does this mean that he or she will actually get a higher position? Give your reason.

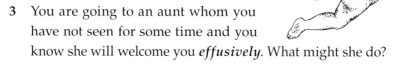

3 You are going to an aunt whom you have not seen for some time and you know she will welcome you *effusively*. What might she do?

4 'The riot should have been stopped by the police at its *inception*.' When should the police have acted?

5 A woman in a novel was described as *lachrymose*. What kind of a person was she?

6 'The house was furnished in a *minimalist* style.' Would it be cluttered or bare?

7 Give an example of a *nocturnal* animal.

8 If a speaker is *verbose*, you will probably not enjoy listening to him. Why not? What would happen if his speech were reported *verbatim*?

9 'In such rough seas the accident was *inevitable*.' What does this mean?

10 Translate the words below and say which is the odd one out.

   precātus   adeptus   dēceptus   ingressus

Check

Language test

1 Translate.

Modestus, tabernam ingressus, Vilbiam vīdit. illa, Modestum cōnspicāta, statim eum amāvit.

'vīnum, puella!' inquit Modestus.

Modestus, haec verba locūtus, cōnsēdit. Vilbia, ā Modestō dēlectāta, vīnum effūdit. Modestus, vīnum adeptus,

'dēliciae meae', inquit, 'quam pulchra es! ego tē cognōscere velim.'

Vilbia, in culīnam regressa,

'ō dea Venus!' inquit. 'ego, tē saepe precāta, grātiās maximās agō, quod hunc virum mīrābilem mihi mīsistī.'

There are six perfect active participles in this passage and one perfect passive participle. List them.

2 Translate the following sentences in your head. Then write down a translation for the words in **bold type**.

a Memor **nimium vīnī** saepe bibēbat.

b difficile est deae **virum octōgintā annōrum** sānāre.

c amīcī thermās **tacitē** intrāvērunt.

d Cephalus **aliquid novī** Memorī nūntiāvit.

e Latrō, **homō minimae prūdentiae**, fīliās suās semper vituperābat.

f Vilbia **virum pulchriōrem** quam Modestum numquam vīderat.

Check

Revision

Nouns: genitive and dative cases pp. 146–7

Using the table of first, second and third declension nouns to help you, give the Latin for the words in italics in the following sentences.

1 The soldier gave jewels *to the girl*.

2 The *citizen's* anger was intense.

3 The thief offered a big bribe *to the merchant*.

4 I shall talk to the *boy's* parents.

5 The master gave new clothes *to the slave*.

Now change the Latin words you have written into the plural.

Imperatives p. 157

Revise the forms of the imperative in paragraph 3.

> Remember that a negative command is expressed by **nōlī** (singular) or **nōlīte** (plural) and the infinitive.

Translate the following sentences, which are taken from **amor omnia vincit**.

1 tacē!

2 stā prope fontem deae!

3 venī ad mē!

4 nōlī mē interficere!

5 nōlī lacrimāre!

Now change the commands into the plural.

Comparatives and superlatives pp. 150–1

Para. 1   Study the forms in the table and note especially the superlative forms of **pulcher** and **facilis**. Using paragraph 1 as a guide, fill in the missing words below.

Adjective	Comparative	Superlative
gravis	....	....
heavy	*heavier*	*very heavy*
perfidus	perfidior	....
....	....	....
difficilis	....	....
difficult	....	*very difficult*
potēns	potentior	....
powerful	....	....
celer	celerior	....
....	*quicker*	....

Para. 2 Learn the forms of the irregular comparatives and superlatives. Then, without looking at paragraph 2, test yourself by filling in the correct English and Latin words, e.g. to ameliorate a situation is to make it better, **melior**.

Latin

a A *malefactor* is someone who does something _____. _____

b An *optimist* always looks at the _____ aspects. _____

c *Magnitude* shows how _____ a thing is. _____

d If a word is in the *plural*, you know it means _____ than one. _____

e The company tried to *minimise* the danger so that everyone would think the risk was _____. _____

f A *multiplex* cinema has _____ screens. _____

Para. 3 Translate.

Para. 4 Read and translate the examples.
Check

Progress record
Textbook pp. 21–36   Student Study Book pp. 16–27

Stage 22 dēfīxiō	Done	Revised	Any problems?
Model sentences			
Vilbia			
Modestus			
About the language 1: perfect active participles			
amor omnia vincit: scaena prīma			
amor omnia vincit: scaena secunda			
amor omnia vincit: scaena tertia			
About the language 2: more about the genitive			
Magic and curses			
Word patterns: more adjectives and adverbs			
Practising the language			
Vocabulary checklist 22			
Language test			
Revision			

Stage 23 haruspex

Cogidubnus, hoping for a cure, goes to the temple of Sulis Minerva to offer the sacrifice of a lamb to the goddess. The lamb is killed and Memor, the haruspex (soothsayer), steps forward to inspect the entrails of the dead animal to see if the omens are favourable. He is horrified by what he sees.

Picture p. 37

In this carving a bull has just been sacrificed and a haruspex (on the left, wearing a toga) is inspecting the animal's entrails. Notice the man carrying an axe and a bucket who has just killed the bull. We shall study this picture in more detail later in the Stage.

in thermīs I p. 38

Read lines 1–10.

1 In lines 1–5, what description are we given of

   a the temple

   b the altar?

2 Where was the ceremony taking place?

3 In lines 3–6 what showed the importance of

   a Quintus

   b the king and his chieftains

   c Memor?

4 **quī iam tremēbat** (line 9). Why do you think that Memor was acting like this?

   Clue: What job had Salvius imposed on Memor in Stage 21?

5 From lines 1–10 write down

   a the noun and perfect passive participle pair

   b TWO noun and present participle pairs

   c TWO nouns in the genitive case.

Read lines 11–20.

6 'iecur est līvidum' (line 12). What did the priest think this signified? Which Latin word showed that he expected Memor to agree with him?

7 Did Memor agree with him (lines 15–16)? Give a reason.

8 How did Memor interpret to Cogidubnus the result of the sacrifice (lines 18–19)?

9 Translate the last line.

10 From lines 11–20 write down

a TWO pronouns in the dative case

b TWO relative clauses

c a perfect active participle.

Further work You have just translated line 20 and will have noticed the order of words in the sentence. The accusatives **rēgem** and **prīncipēs** come before the nominative **Memor**. You have met sentences like these before and they will become increasingly common in the Course. Here are some further examples. In each sentence highlight or underline the nominative and then translate the sentence.

1 āram omnēs aspiciēbant.

2 agnam sacerdōs sacrificāvit.

3 iecur agnae haruspex īnspexit.

4 nōnne mortem hoc significat?

Check

Roman religion pp. 48–9

Read the text and study the pictures. Look again at the picture at the bottom of p. 48.

1 How can you tell that this is an important sacrifice?

2 Can you spot the man who is to kill the animals?

3 What are the people in the procession wearing on their heads? How is the bull decorated?

4 The emperor has taken incense from the box held by the man on the far right and is burning the incense on the altar. Do you know, or can you guess, why he is doing this?

Check

in thermīs II pp. 39–40

1 Read lines 1–15 and explain the reasons for these words or phrases. In each case mention the persons concerned.

Line	Word or phrase	Reason
3	attonitus	
6	cum magnā difficultāte	
7	maximus clāmor	
12	anxius	

2 The places marked on the plan below have all been mentioned in the story **in thermīs**. Can you identify them?

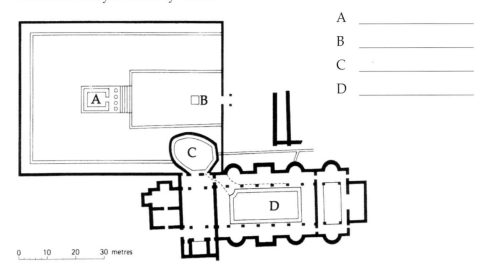

A _____

B _____

C _____

D _____

0   10   20   30 metres

3 At this point in the story the **pōculum** becomes very significant. Read lines 16–25 and then write down what each of the characters did with, or about, the **pōculum**.

Line	Character	Actions
16	Cephalus	
16–17	Cogidubnus	
18	Quintus	
19–21	Quintus	
22	Quintus	
22–3	Cephalus	
24–5	Dumnorix	

4 Read the rest of the story and answer the questions.

    a 'num aquam bibere timēs?' (line 27). Explain what Dumnorix meant when he asked this question. What tone of voice do you think he used?

    b Why would Cephalus' behaviour have aroused suspicion (lines 28–9)?

    c Who is described as **immōtus** (line 29)? Why was he in this state?

    d What part did the **prīncipēs** play in the final outcome (lines 29–31)?

    e Which word in the last sentence tells you that the poison was effective?

Further work In lines 4–5 Quintus says

    'hae thermae maiōrēs sunt quam thermae Pompēiānae!'

What would he have meant if he had said

    'hae thermae minōrēs/meliōrēs/peiōrēs sunt quam thermae Pompēiānae.'

Or, 'hae thermae sunt minimae/optimae/pessimae'?

Check

Picture p. 40

You can see the original position of the Gorgon's head in the drawing on p. 42. Gorgons are often portrayed as monstrous females by Greek and Roman artists, like the Greek one on the right. At Bath the Celtic sculptor has carved a male face surrounded by the usual snaky hair.

About the language 1: more about participles p. 41

This note brings together what you have already learnt about participles.

Paras 1–3 Read. List the three different sorts of participles you have met so far.

Paras 4–5 Translate the sentences and complete the exercise as instructed.

Check

Roman religion continued pp. 50–3

Read the text and study the pictures. Then answer the following questions.

1 You are probably familiar with the Greek and Roman family of gods and goddesses from the previous books in this Course and from myths and legends.

Complete the grid by matching the Greek deities and their characteristics and spheres of influence with their Roman equivalents.

Hera

Athene

Hermes

Zeus

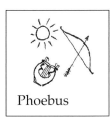
Phoebus

Roman deity	Greek deity	Characteristics, spheres of influence
Jupiter		
Juno		
Minerva		
Ceres		
Apollo		
Mars		
Mercury		

Ares

Demeter

2 You can often recognise paintings and statues of gods and goddesses by the objects associated with them. For example, Minerva is often portrayed with the Gorgon's head on her cloak or shield and an owl. Can you identify the gods below from these emblems: thunderbolt; lyre; herald's staff twined with snakes?

a  b  c

_____   _____   _____

3 Some of the names of gods and goddesses have come into the English language. For example, Vulcan, the god of metal working, was said to have his forge under the earth, since flames and molten rock sometimes erupted from it. The study of volcanoes is therefore called vulcanology. Complete the following.

a Skills in combat and defence are called _____ arts.

b Grain crops are sometimes called _____ .

c Someone with a cheerful disposition, like Jove (another name for Jupiter), is said to be _____ .

Check

epistula Cephalī p. 42

Read the Latin text alongside the translation below. Then cover up the translation. Re-read the Latin and answer the questions.

Translation

After Cephalus died, his slave handed to the king a letter written by Cephalus himself:

'King Cogidubnus, you are in very great danger. Memor is mad. He wants your death. He has ordered me to do the deed. I obeyed Memor against my will. Perhaps you do not believe me. But I should like to tell you the whole story.

When you came to these baths, seeking a cure, Memor summoned me to his villa. Having entered the villa, I found Memor terrified.

"The Emperor wants the death of Cogidubnus", he said. "I order you to manage this task. I order you to prepare poison. For Cogidubnus is a man of evil character."

I replied to Memor,

"You are making a big mistake. Cogidubnus is a man of excellent character. I do not wish to do such a thing."

Memor said angrily,

"Scoundrel! You are my freedman. You must carry out my orders. Why are you obstructing me?"

King Cogidubnus, for a long time I stubbornly refused. For a long time I recounted your acts of kindness. At last Memor summoned a guard who beat me. When I had been almost killed by the guard, I finally gave in to Memor.

Having returned to my house, I reluctantly prepared the poison. However, I wrote this letter and handed it to a faithful slave. I ordered the slave to hand over the letter to you. I ask for pardon, although I have planned a wicked crime. Memor forced me to carry this out. You ought to punish Memor, not me.'

Questions

1 In the box below are parts of the conversation Cephalus says he had with Memor. Compare these with what actually happened in **Memor rem suscipit II** (p. 11) and say whether they are true (T) or false (F), giving your reason.

Line	Statement	T/F	Reason
3	Memor īnsānit.		
9	"Imperātor mortem Cogidubnī cupit", inquit (Memor).		
10	"iubeō tē venēnum parāre."		
12–13	Memorī respondī, "longē errās. Cogidubnus est vir ingeniī optimī."		
19–20	Memor custōdem arcessīvit, quī mē verberāvit.		
24	Memor coēgit mē hanc rem efficere.		

2 Why do you think Cephalus wrote this letter?

Check

About the language 2: the plural of neuter nouns p. 43

Paras 1–2 Study the forms of the nominative and accusative cases of neuter nouns and learn them. What do these cases have in common? What do neuter plurals have in common?

Para. 3 Translate the sentences.

Further work Translate these two pairs of sentences.

1 a templa sunt splendida.

   b puella est laetissima.

2 a templa in Britanniā saepe vīsitāvī.

   b puella mātrem saepe vīsitāvit.

Write down the case and number of **templa** and **puella** in each sentence.

Check

Britannia perdomita pp. 44–5

The play divides into three parts. Read each part and answer the questions before moving on to the next part.

Lines 1–11, questions 1–4. Salvius and Memor are alarmed at the approach of Cogidubnus and his band of armed men.

Lines 12–24, questions 5–8. Cogidubnus accuses Memor of plotting to kill him.

Lines 25–42, questions 9–15. Salvius condemns Cogidubnus.

Check

Further work

1 Translate into good English.

   a id quod dīcis absurdum est (line 15).

   b Cephalus homō magnae prūdentiae erat (line 17).

   c Memorem ē cūrā thermārum iam dēmōvī (line 26).

   d nūllī perfidiōrēs sunt quam Rōmānī (lines 36–7).

2 Find in the play:

   a a verb in the 2nd person singular, perfect tense

   b a noun and perfect passive participle pair

   c a noun and perfect active participle pair

   d a neuter plural noun.

3 After reading this play and from what you have learnt earlier about him, do you:

   a feel sorry for Cogidubnus

   b think he deserved his fate?

   Give reasons for your answer.

Check

Picture p. 45

A bronze coin of the Emperor Antoninus Pius, AD 154–5, showing the sad figure of Britannia sitting on a pile of rocks. It was possibly minted to celebrate the building of the Antonine Wall in Scotland after a rebellion in AD 154. The inscription reads BRITANNIA C. The C is all that remains of COS IIII, which dates the coin to the emperor's fourth consulship.

The coin opposite also celebrates the Romans' victory over the Britons. This was minted about AD 46 just after Claudius' invasion. It shows the emperor in a four-horse chariot holding a sceptre. DE BRITANNIS means *(triumph) over the Britons.* **dē** can be used in this sense as well as in its more common meanings *down from* and *about.*

Word patterns: verbs and nouns p. 46

Para. 1 Study the forms carefully, noting that the nouns are formed from the perfect passive participle.

Paras 2, 3, 5 Complete as instructed.

Para. 4 Read the instructions and then in the table write down the perfect passive participle and infinitive of the Latin verbs from which the English nouns are formed. The first one has been done for you.

English noun	Perfect passive participle	Infinitive
demonstrator	dēmōnstrātus	dēmōnstrāre
curator		
navigator		
narrator		
tractor		
doctor		

Do you know what the caption means?

caveat ēmptor.

Further work Complete this table in the same way by filling in the correct verb forms for the Latin nouns in paragraph 3.

Latin noun	Perfect passive participle	Infinitive
dēfēnsor		
vēnditor		
prōditor		
amātor		

The letters F.D. (an abbreviation of FIDEI DEFENSOR) appear on British coins. Do you know what the phrase means?

Check

Practising the language p. 47

Ex. 1 This exercise gives you more practice with all the verb tenses.

Ex. 2 In this exercise you will practise the perfect participles which you met in Stages 21 and 22. Go through the list of participles first, translating them and noting whether they are active or passive. Then do the exercise as instructed.
Check

Vocabulary pp. 168–9

Before learning the checklist, revise the way that verbs are listed. Then work through the examples in paragraph 5 on p. 169 and read paragraph 6.
Check

Vocabulary checklist 23 p. 54

Learn the checklist and answer the questions.

1 In a debate, if your opponent *cedes* a point to you, why would you be pleased?

2 A *curator*
   a is a clergyman
   b cares for the sick
   c looks after a museum or art collection.

3 When people are presented with *honorary* degrees, what does it mean?

4 If you were taking a course in *elocution* would you be learning to
   a become an electrician
   b rehouse people
   c speak effectively?

5 The chairman of a society was given a *mandate* to vote for the members. What does this mean?

6 What is a *modus vivendi*?

7 'The mantelpiece was crowded with *ornaments*.' What is the main purpose of *ornaments*?

8 On his return from hospital the patient's condition quickly *regressed* to its earlier state. Would his family be encouraged by this?

9 What is the original meaning of *science*?

10 With what creatures is *venom* usually associated? Why?

11 What is the difference in meaning between **pārēre** and **parāre**?

12 What do these words mean: **umquam, enim, tālis, nimium**?
Check

Language test

1 Fill in the gaps in the table below. The forms given you for one word may help you with other words. If you need further help, consult table 1, pp. 146–7.

Nominative singular	Accusative singular	Accusative plural	Gender
toga		togās	feminine
rēx	rēgem		
dōnum		dōna	
īnsula	īnsulam		
custōs		custōdēs	
flūmen		flūmina	neuter
mandātum	mandātum		
lībertus		lībertōs	

2 Translate the following sentences which summarise the story of the sacrifice and the attempted murder of Cogidubnus. Then pick out the noun and participle pairs and state whether they are singular or plural.

a prīncipēs, cum rēge ingressī, prō templō sedēbant.

b sacerdōtēs, victimam dūcentēs, ad āram prōcessērunt.

c Memor, prope āram stāns, ōmina īnspexit.

d rēx prīncipēsque, Memorem secūtī, thermās intrāvērunt.

e rēx, ē balneō ēgressus, vestīmenta induit.

f Cephalus prope fontem stābat, pōculum tenēns.

g spectātōrēs, hoc cōnspicātī, stābant immōtī.

h prīncipēs lībertum resistentem comprehendērunt.

i Cephalus, ā prīncipibus coāctus, venēnum hausit.

j lībertus, vehementer tremēns, mortuus prōcubuit.

 Check

Revision

Verbs

As you know, if you are familiar with the main parts of a verb which are set out in the checklists, you should be able to recognise all the different forms of the verb.

The main parts of the following verbs are in **Vocabulary checklist 23**. Translate these forms and state the tenses.

Verb	Translation	Tense
gessī		
ōrnat		
scīverant		
pārēbās		
cēdunt		
iēcistī		
gerimus		
ōrnābātis		
cessērunt		
sciēbam		

Check

Pronouns I p. 152

Para. 1 Revise the singular and plural forms of **ego** and **tū** and read the note below the table.

Para. 2 Learn the forms of **sē** and study the examples.

The same forms are used for masculine and feminine singular and plural.

Further work Write down the Latin for the words in **bold type** in the following sentences.

1 He gave many books **to us**.

2 We shall see **you** all in the theatre.

3 The woman bought the dress **for herself**.

4 Friend, why do **you** blame **me**?

5 **We** wanted to go **with you**, Modestus.

6 They refused to take **us with them**.

Check

Progress record

Textbook pp. 37–54   Student Study Book pp. 29–39

Stage 23 haruspex	Done	Revised	Any problems?
in thermīs I			
Roman religion			
in thermīs II			
About the language 1: more about participles			
Roman religion continued			
epistula Cephalī			
About the language 2: the plural of neuter nouns			
Britannia perdomita			
Word patterns: verbs and nouns			
Practising the language			
Vocabulary			
Vocabulary checklist 23			
Language test			
Revision			

Stage 24 fuga

Modestus and Strythio leave Bath for the legionary fortress at Chester. Perhaps their leave has run out or Modestus no longer wants to stay after his ordeal in the sacred spring.

Can you identify Modestus and Strythio in the drawing? From the previous stories did you expect them to look like this?

Picture p. 55

This mosaic of galloping horses and their riders has been chosen to illustrate the title of the Stage, **fuga**. You will find out later in this Stage who was forced to flee and why.

The mosaic shows two Tunisian huntsmen riding bare-back without stirrups in the usual Roman way.

in itinere p. 56

Read lines 1–8 then answer the questions.

1 Which word in the first sentence tells you how the friends were travelling?

2 Why did the river present problems? What was the horse's reaction?

3 What was Modestus' solution? Why was it not successful?

4 When did the horse go across the bridge?

Write out a translation of lines 9–13.

> Note the new meaning of **cum** (line 11).
> **mediīs ex undīs** (line 12) is another way of saying **ex mediīs undīs**.

5 To whom is the last sentence addressed?
Check

Roman bridges

The numerous Roman bridges which have survived until today are impressive stone structures with one or more arches, like the sketch on the next page. The bridge in the story you have just read was obviously very different. In fact, many Roman bridges were modest wooden structures which would need repairing or replacing from time to time.

We may imagine that Modestus and Strythio came to a wooden bridge that had been built thirty years before by the Romans after the conquest or had been erected by British tribesmen and was now in need of repair.

The picture question below tests your knowledge of words mostly connected with the story.

Label the diagram using the correct letters to stand for the Latin words.

P   pōns   R   rīpa
U   unda   A   aqua
F   fōns   M   mare
FL flūmen

Check

Quīntus cōnsilium capit pp. 58–9

This story takes place after the show-down between Salvius and Cogidubnus in the last Stage. Cogidubnus is disillusioned and in despair because of the treachery of the Romans, but worse is to follow.

Read lines 1–16 and answer questions 1–6 on p. 59.

Further work Write down:

1 TWO nouns in the genitive plural.

2 TWO nouns in the genitive singular.

3 TWO pairs of nouns or pronouns and perfect passive participles.

4 TWO imperatives (words which give an order to someone).

Read the rest of the story and answer questions 7–12.
Check

Further questions 1 What do you think Salvius intended to do with Cogidubnus?

2 How would you describe the behaviour of Dumnorix in this story? How does it compare with what you know about him already? Clues: Think about the part he played in preventing the poisoning of Cogidubnus (Stage 23), in the boat-race (Book II, Stage 15) and in the incident of the bear (Stage 16).

3 'tū anteā eum servāvistī' (lines 15–16). On which two previous occasions did Quintus save Cogidubnus' life? Use the clues given in question 2 to help you.

4 Look at the picture. Pick out and translate the phrase in the last sentence which refers to it.

Check

About the language 1: *cum* and the pluperfect subjunctive p. 60

Paras 1–2   Study the examples and read the notes. The new verb form, the subjunctive, is found with certain words. **cum**, meaning *when*, is the first one of these you have met.

Para. 3   Translate the sentences.

Para. 4   Revise the ordinary pluperfect forms, noting the ending **-erat**, and then study how the pluperfect subjunctive is formed.

> The meaning of the pluperfect subjunctive, when it is found with **cum**, is exactly the same as the ordinary pluperfect.

Further work   1   With the help of the table on p. 60, fill in the missing parts of the pluperfect subjunctives below.

Pluperfect	*Pluperfect subjunctive*	
singular	*singular*	*plural*
ōrnāverat	ōrnāv.........................	ōrnāvissent
monuerat	.........................isset	monu........................
ēlēgerat	ēlēg..........................	....
scīverat	....	....

2   Turn back to the story on p. 58; pick out and translate the three examples of **cum** and the pluperfect subjunctive.

Check

Salvius cōnsilium cognōscit pp. 61–2

1   Read lines 1–6 and explain who carried out these actions and for what reason.

Line	Action	By whom	Reason
1–2	contenderent		
2–3	Dumnorigem … quaerēbant		
4	vehementer saeviēbat		
6	Belimicum … arcessīvit		

2   For lines 7–30 your job is to put a translation of the conversations in the boxes. Read the rest of the Latin with the help of the translations below.

Salvius said,

Having gone out with many soldiers, Belimicus began to search carefully throughout the town. Meanwhile Salvius was anxiously awaiting his return. When Salvius was thinking over the problem (with himself), Belimicus suddenly returned triumphant. He dragged Quintus' slave into the middle of the hall.

Salvius, having turned to the quivering slave, said,

> (blank box)

The slave, who, having suffered many tortures, was hardly able to say anything, said,

> (blank box)

He said again,

> (blank box)

When he had heard this, Belimicus drew his sword and held it to the slave's throat. He said,

> (blank box)

The slave, who was now despairing for his life, said in a whisper,

> (blank box)

Salvius said,

> (blank box)

3 Read the rest of the story. Decide whether these statements are true (T) or false (F). For those you decide are false, give your reason.

  a Before he spoke, Salvius gave Belimicus a reward.

  b Belimicus had to leave with thirty horsemen and arrest Quintus and Dumnorix.

  c The slave had been right to despair of his life.

  d Salvius' secretary was ordered to convey a letter to Agricola.

  e Belimicus, Quintus and Dumnorix were followed for three days.

f The horsemen attacked and surrounded Quintus and Dumnorix.

g Before he died, Dumnorix was trampled by the horses.

h Quintus was not able to escape because he was badly wounded.

	T/F	Reason (if false)
a		
b		
c		
d		
e		
f		
g		
h		

Check

Picture p. 62

This shows the Roman road looking south, so you have to imagine Quintus and Dumnorix travelling north between the two ranges of hills towards the camera. The map on the right shows their route from Bath to Chester via Corinium (Cirencester), Glevum (Gloucester) and Viroconium (Wroxeter). For a complete map of the major roads in Roman Britain see p. 139. There were several smaller roads that linked Glevum to the road going north to Viroconium.

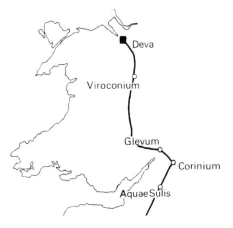

The route from Bath to Chester

Travel and communication pp. 66–7

Read the text and study the pictures. In the top picture on p. 66, the surface of the road has been worn away or robbed by later builders. Turn back to p. 57 for another view of this road.

Further work **1** The distance from Bath to Chester is about 160 miles. Using the information on p. 66, answer these questions.

    a How far do you think Quintus and Dumnorix travelled in the four days (allowing them a day's start on Belimicus and his cavalry) before they were caught? Give your reasons.

    b How long do you think it would take Modestus and Strythio to travel from Bath to Chester? Think of their characters and remember that they had only one horse between them.

2 List the different kinds of material you would have to order, as a Roman engineer, to construct a road.

Check

Roman transport

Note the Roman milestone in the main picture on p. 67. It shows the distance from Igel in Germany, where the carving was found, to the nearby city of Trier. L. IIII = 4 leugae (4 Gallic leagues, about 8 km). See the milestone on p. 70 and the note on p. 48 of this *Student Study Book*.

In the picture at bottom left two passengers travel inside a coach of the Imperial Post, while on top is the driver and a public official, whose importance is shown by the staff of office held by the attendant sitting back to back with him. (You will read about the Imperial Post in the next section.) At bottom right the two oxen pull a cart containing the complete skin of an ox. This was normally used to transport wine in bulk.

About the language 2: *cum* and the imperfect subjunctive p. 63

Paras 1 and 2 Read and note carefully the different translations of the pluperfect and imperfect subjunctives. They have the same meanings as those of the ordinary pluperfect and imperfect tenses.

Para. 3 Translate the sentences.

Para. 4 Study the note. Why do you think the infinitive is given in the table?

Further work
1 In paragraph 3 pick out the verbs that are in the imperfect subjunctive.

2 On pp. 61–2 find and translate the three sentences containing **cum** and the imperfect subjunctive.

3 In the table below, write down the infinitives of the verbs listed, using the **Vocabulary** to help you. Then form the 3rd person singular of the imperfect subjunctive. The first one is done for you.

Present tense	Infinitive	Imperfect subjunctive
adiuvō	adiuvāre	adiuvāret
iubeō	iubēre	iubēret
scrībō	scrībere	scrīberet
scio	scīre	scīret
capiō	capere	caperet
eō	īre	īret
possum	posse	posset
nōlō	nōlle	nōllet

Check

Travel and communication continued pp. 68–9

Read pp. 68–9 and study the pictures. The tugboat on p. 69 would have towed merchant ships from the port of Ostia at the mouth of the Tiber up river to Rome. Note the oarsmen, the big steering oar and the towing rope on the left.

In the lower picture does the lighthouse remind you of any other you have seen? What do you think the purpose of the flags is?

1 Write down five different kinds of traveller you might have seen on a road in Britain. What methods of travel might they have used? (You may need to revise what you read on p. 66.)

2 Imagine that you are Quintus travelling from Egypt to Roman Britain, partly by land and partly by sea. What preparations would you make for your journeys? Remember that you are a rich young man and would be carrying money and expensive presents (like silver tripods) as well as your baggage.

3 You are the captain of a merchant ship and have just completed a voyage. Write up your log book, using the information on pp. 68–9. For cargoes and routes, see Book II, pp. 86–7. If you wish to describe a storm at sea, you could read the experiences of St Paul (about AD 60) in the Acts of the Apostles, chapter 27.

Check

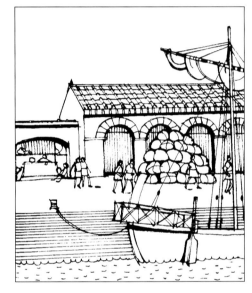

Word patterns: opposites p. 64

Paras 1–2 Read, and fill in the missing words.

Para. 3 Do the exercise as instructed.

Para. 4 Work out the meaning of the words, and then write down their Latin opposites.
Check

Practising the language p. 65

Ex. 1 Here you need to concentrate on choosing the correct case of the adjective.
Check

If you have made more than two mistakes, revise the forms of the adjective on p. 148.

Ex. 2 Read the directions carefully and study the example. Then write out the sentences as instructed.
Check

Vocabulary checklist 24 p. 70

Learn the checklist and answer the questions.

1 Nelson was famous for his *audacity* in battle. How did he behave?

2 *Incarceration* in the Tower of London often ended in execution. What does incarceration mean?

3 **Comprehendere** can also mean *understand*. How is this connected to its other meanings? What is the word derived from it in English?

4 Give the different meanings of **cum** in this sentence: **rēx, cum Rōmānōs vituperāvisset, cum prīncipibus suīs discessit.**

5 Look at the picture and these words: **equus, equitāre, eques**. Which is a man, which an animal and which an action?

6 The novel was published *posthumously*. What does this mean and what is the connection with **humī**?

7 To climb Everest requires *maximum* effort from all members of the team. Can you think of another word for maximum?

8 What is a *pontoon*?

9 We may be making the *transition* to a period of global warming. Explain the derivation of transition.

10 If you were asked to *verify* a statement, what would you be expected to do?

Check

Picture p. 70

This milestone was erected in the reign of the Emperor Trajan. It is inscribed: CAESAR IMP NERVAE F TRAIANUS GERM DACIC (*Trajan, Caesar and Emperor, conqueror of Germany and Dacia, son of Nerva*). Dacia was a province in eastern Europe, roughly where Romania is today. The milestone marks the 75th mile of the Via Traiana from Beneventum in south Italy.

Language test

1 Complete the sentences with the correct word from the brackets and then translate the sentences.

   a cum mīlitēs oppidum _____, omnēs cīvēs maximē timēbant. (cēpisset, cēpissent)

   b cum dominus haec verba _____, servī lībertīque dīligenter labōrāre coepērunt. (dīxisset, dīxissent)

   c lēgātus, cum centuriōnem ad sē _____, eī praemium dedit. (arcessīvisset, arcessīvissent)

   d rēx et amīcī, cum ad aulam _____, cēnam splendidissimam cōnsūmpsērunt. (pervēnisset, pervēnissent)

   e cum mīlitēs per urbem _____, fūr in silvā sē cēlābat. (quaereret, quaererent)

   f puerī, cum ad theātrum _____, multōs dēnāriōs in viā invēnērunt. (contenderet, contenderent)

2 Translate the sentences.

   a equitēs, prīncipem comprehendere iussī, mandāta statim effēcērunt.

   b vir maximae virtūtis es. nōnne rēgem amīcōsque servāre vīs?

   c verba Salviī audīvistis?

   d nimium labōris habēmus. ā dominō verberātī, in hāc vīllā manēre nōlumus.

   e in hortō rēgis ambulāns, multōs flōrēs pulcherrimōs cōnspexī.

   f agnam, ad āram ductam, omnēs spectābant.

In the sentences above there are two neuter plural nouns. What are they?

Check

Revision

Pronouns II p. 153

Revise the forms of **hic**, **ille** and **is**, and then give the Latin for the words in *italic type* in paragraph 4.

Check

Fourth and fifth declension nouns pp. 146–7

In many stories you have already met fourth and fifth declension nouns and have had no difficulty translating them because many of their endings are the same as nouns in other declensions. Study the tables and then write down:

1 Two cases of **manus** and **servus** that have the same endings.

2 Three cases of **diēs** and **mercātor** that have the same endings.

3 Two cases of **genū, templum** and **nōmen** that have the same ending.

4 The difference between the nominative singular and nominative plural of **manus**.

Do the exercise in paragraph 4 as instructed.

There are relatively few fourth and fifth declension nouns and you will be relieved that there are no more declensions to learn.

Dative case The following sentences all contain a dative case. Translate the sentences.

1 rem dēnique Salviō nūntiāvērunt.

2 neque Dumnorigī neque Quīntō crēdō.

3 facile est nōbīs servōs torquēre.

4 Quīntus virō potentī obstāre temptat.

5 mihi resistere nōn potest.

6 servum carnificibus trādidit.

7 deinde scrībam arcessīvit cui epistulam dictāvit.

How do you account for the dative case in sentences 2, 4 and 5?

If you are unsure of the endings of the dative case, see pp. 146–7 for the nouns, p. 152 for pronouns and p. 155 for the relative pronoun in sentence 7.

Check

Progress record   Textbook pp. 55–70   Student Study Book pp. 41–50

Stage 24 fuga	Done	Revised	Any problems?
in itinere			
Roman bridges			
Quīntus cōnsilium capit			
About the language 1: *cum* and the pluperfect subjunctive			
Salvius cōnsilium cognōscit			
Travel and communication			
About the language 2: *cum* and the imperfect subjunctive			
Travel and communication continued			
Word patterns: opposites			
Practising the language			
Vocabulary checklist 24			
Language test			
Revision			

Stage 25 mīlitēs

Modestus and Strythio, soldiers of the Second
Legion, have now returned to their camp at
Chester (Deva). This Stage tells you of another
of their misadventures and introduces you to
other soldiers in the legion.

Picture p. 71

This is part of a carving on the base of the Column of Antoninus Pius, a later
emperor. It shows the parade of soldiers after his death, celebrating his deification
(i.e. being made into a god).

You will learn about the arms and armour of the soldiers later in the Stage, but
note that all the soldiers in this carving have beards; this was the fashion from
the time of the Emperor Hadrian.

Model sentences pp. 72–3

Read and study the pictures; then answer the following questions.

Dēvae	*at Chester*
legiōnis: legiō	*legion*
castra	*camp*
ignōtum: ignōtus	*unknown*

Sentences 1   **a**   What was the soldier doing?

       b   What did he suddenly notice?

       c   What question did the soldier ask? Write it down in Latin and
translate it.

       d   When he received no reply, what did the soldier do?

       e   What was the reaction?

Sentences 2   **a**   When the soldier chased and overpowered the young man,
what was his next question? Write it down in Latin and
translate it.

       b   Complete this sentence and write it down.

           The young man did not want to say _____.

       c   What happened next?

Sentences 3 a Who did the centurion say the young man was?

  b How had he come to this conclusion?

  c What did the centurion ask the soldier? Write down the question in Latin and English.

  d Translate **tum mīles explicāvit quō modō iuvenem cēpisset**.

Sentences 4 a What did the centurion ask the young man? Write down the question in Latin and English.

  b Which Latin word indicates that the young man did not reply to the question?

  c Complete the translation of this sentence.

  The centurion, when _____

  _____, ordered the soldier to take him to jail.

Now read the last paragraph.

  a When did the young man finally reply?

  b What TWO pieces of information do we learn about him from his reply?

  c **vōbīs nōn decōrum est mē in carcere tenēre**. What did the young man object to?

  d Why was the centurion very glad to see the young man?

  e Why do you think the centurion describes the cell as **optimam**?

 Check

Study this line drawing and the one on the previous page.

1 How does the uniform of the centurion differ from that of the legionary soldier?

2 What does the centurion hold to symbolise his authority?

3 Which two pieces of equipment does the legionary soldier not have with him in this drawing?

 Check

Strȳthiō p. 74

There are two ways of dealing with this story, depending on the time available. If you are short of time, turn to p. 55 and follow the directions for Option 2.

Option 1

If you have the time, read the complete story and answer the following questions:

1 Where is the camp?

2 Why does the optio summon Strythio (line 3)?

3 How does Strythio respond to the summons?

4 What order of the centurion does the optio pass on to Strythio?

5 What is Strythio's reaction?

6 Who else has the centurion given an order to (lines 10–11)?

7 How does Strythio's attitude change from lines 12–13 to lines 16–18?

8 In the job assigned to Modestus and Strythio, what quality is particularly important, according to the optio (lines 21–5)?

9 **fortissimī sumus** (line 27). What example does Strythio give of this in lines 27–9?

10 In the table below are some lines of the dialogue you have read. Look back over the story and suggest the tone of voice in which each of these lines is delivered.

Line	Dialogue	Tone
6–7	mī Strȳthiō, quamquam occupātissimus es, …	
10	tacē!	
12	deōs testēs faciō. innocentēs sumus.	
14	caudex! tacē!	
19	(susurrāns) difficile est mihi hoc crēdere.	
20	quid dīcis?	

Check

Further work   1 Translate the following sentences which are taken from the story.

    a Strȳthiōnem, iam Dēvam regressum, cōnspicit.

    b Modestum quaerō.

    c deōs testēs faciō.

    d nūllum facinus commīsimus.

    e rem nunc intellegō.

    Can you see what pattern all these sentences have in common?

    2 Suppose the optio and Strythio were talking to more than one person. What would be the plural of the following imperatives? If in doubt, turn to p. 157, paragraph 3.

    a hūc venī!

    b nōlī mē vexāre!

    c tacē!

Option 2

If you are short of time, you could just translate the following shortened form of this story in your head and do questions 1 and 2 in the **Further work** above.

(optiō per castra ambulat. Strȳthiōnem, iam Dēvam regressum, cōnspicit.)

optiō: heus, Strȳthiō! hūc venī! tibi aliquid dīcere volō.

Strȳthiō: nōlī mē vexāre! occupātus sum. Modestum quaerō, quod puella eum exspectat.

optiō: centuriō tē iubet ad carcerem statim festīnāre.

Strȳthiō: īnsānit centuriō! innocēns sum!

optiō: tacē! centuriō Modestum quoque iussit ad carcerem festīnāre.

Strȳthiō: deōs testēs faciō! nūllum facinus commīsimus!

optiō: caudex! tacē! centuriō vōs ambōs carcerem custōdīre iussit! inter captīvōs est Vercobrix, iuvenis magnae dignitātis, cuius pater est prīnceps Deceanglōrum. necesse est vōbīs Vercobrigem dīligentissimē custōdīre.

Strȳthiō: nōlī anxius esse, mī optiō. rem nunc intellegō. nōbīs nihil difficile est, quod fortissimī sumus.

(exeunt. optiō centuriōnem quaerit, Strȳthiō amīcum.)

Picture p. 74

Compare this with the line drawing of the tombstone shown here.

1 What two things does the optio hold to suggest that

    a he had authority

    b he was responsible for managing such things as the duty rotas in the legion?

2 You will learn how to interpret the inscription in Stage 28, but in the meantime can you spot

    a his name (part of which will be familiar to you)

    b his rank

    c the number of his legion?

Check

Modestus custōs p. 75

Read the following translation of lines 1–6 with the Latin text:

Having entered the prison, Modestus and Strythio began inspecting the cells in which the prisoners were. Strythio had a writing tablet on which the names of the prisoners were written. Modestus asked him in which cell Vercobrix was imprisoned. Consulting the tablet, Strythio found out where Vercobrix was lying and led Modestus to the cell. When Modestus had arrived at the door of the cell, he stopped, uncertain.

Can you suggest why Modestus **incertus cōnstitit** (line 6)?

Now fill in the missing parts of the translation of lines 7–20:

Strythio said, 'Why are you afraid to enter the cell? The son of the chieftain of the Deceangli is tied up. He can't hurt you.' _____ these words, Modestus _____ exclaimed, 'Blockhead, _____ the son of the chieftain! I stopped because _____. I want you _____!' _____ Strythio _____ the door, Modestus again _____.

    'The cell is dark', said Modestus _____. 'Bring me a lamp.' Strythio, a very patient man, brought a lamp and handed it to his friend. He, _____ the cell, disappeared from sight.

    Vercobrix was lying in the corner of the cell. Modestus, _____, drew his sword. Then, _____, he began to curse Vercobrix. However, Vercobrix could not hear the insults of Modestus because _____.

A spider suddenly appeared. Plot the sequence of actions or reactions in lines 21–3 (translated into English) of the spider and of Modestus, in the boxes below.

	1st action	2nd action	3rd action
spider			
Modestus			

Read lines 24 to the end and answer the questions.

1   Why was Strythio **attonitus** (lines 24–5)?

2   What does Modestus order Strythio to do, and why?

3   **'etiam arāneae eum adiuvant!'** (line 28). How true is this statement?

4   Why do you think Modestus says **'minimē!'** (line 32) in answer to Strythio's question? What explanation does he give for being **pallidus**?

5   What offer does Strythio make (line 33)?

6   Who remains as **custōs** of the jail at the end of the story? How does this contrast with the title of the story? Would you change the title? Give a reason.

Check

Practising the language   p. 80

Do exercise 1 as instructed. Look back at **Modestus custōs**, p. 75, if necessary.

Check

About the language 1: indirect questions   p. 76

Read paragraphs 1–3. Look back at your work on the model sentences and compare the direct and indirect questions. Now translate the examples in paragraph 4.

Further work   Translate each sentence and highlight or underline the indirect question in the Latin and in your translation. Then write in the bubbles in *English* what the direct question would have been. The first one is done for you.

1

mīles explōrātōrem Britannicum rogāvit **cūr prope horreum stāret**.

*The soldier asked the British spy **why he was standing near the granary**.*

2

mīles explōrātōrem rogāvit quō modō castra Rōmāna intrāvisset.

_____

_____

3

centuriō mīlitem rogāvit ubi explōrātōrem
Britannicum invēnisset.

_____

_____

4

centuriō nōn cognōscere poterat quid
explōrātor in castrīs faceret.

_____

_____

Modestus perfuga I p. 77

Translate the sentences below in your head. Then write down in the boxes the
comments or thoughts of Modestus in the story that go with the sentences. If you
like, you could do this in cartoon form, drawing in the scene at the prison and
the figure of Modestus with speech or thought bubbles.

There are no words of Modestus to go in the first box.

1 Modestus, ēgressus ē culīnā ubi cēnam optimam cōnsūmpserat, ad carcerem lentē redībat (lines 1–2).	2 ubi carcerī appropinquāvit, portam apertam vīdit (line 3).

3 carcerem ingressus, portās omnium cellārum apertās invēnit (line 6).	4 Modestus rem anxius cōgitāvit. nesciēbat enim quō captīvī fūgissent; intellegere nōn poterat cūr Strȳthiō abesset (lines 10–11).

Further work From the story pick out two direct questions and two indirect questions and translate them.

	Direct questions	Indirect questions
Latin		
Translation		

Latin		
Translation		

Modestus perfuga II p. 78

Complete this translation of lines 1–11:

Having said these words, Modestus _____.

Someone was trying to open the door of Vercobrix's cell and escape!

'*I must flee from jail*', _____. *Modestus*, _____
_____, *ran to the door of the cell and shut it.*

'*Vercobrix, you must remain in your cell!' shouted Modestus. 'Hurray!*
_____! _____!

Hurray! Now the centurion cannot harm me because _____
_____.'

However, Modestus remained worried; for he did not know _____
_____ *to Strythio. Suddenly he caught sight of* _____
_____.

Write out a translation of lines 12 to the end.

Check

Modestus perfuga III p. 78

Read and answer the questions:

1 How did Modestus begin to avenge Strythio's death (lines 1–2)?

2 What mistake did he make?

3 In line 6 how does Modestus' tone change from **'num vīvus es?'** to **'cūr vīvus es?'**

4 What question did Modestus ask Strythio (line 7)?

5 What answer and explanation did Strythio give?

6 **'quid facere dēbēmus?'** (line 10). What was Strythio's reply? What was his reason?

Check

Further exercise   Based on your reading of all three parts of this story, suggest a reason why Modestus reacted in the various ways described in the table below.

Part and line	Reaction	Reason
I. 3	permōtus	
I. 10	anxius	
I. 15	invītus	
II. 7	euge!	
II. 10	anxius	
II. 13	ēheu!	
III. 1	furēns	
III. 7	sceleste!	
III. 10	ēheu!	
III. 13	ō, quam īnfēlīx sum!	

Check

About the language 2: more about the imperfect and pluperfect subjunctive p. 79

Read paragraphs 1 and 2. Translate the sentences in paragraph 3; then pick out the subjunctives and follow the instructions at the end of the exercise by filling in the table below. The first one is done for you.

Subjunctive	1st singular	1st plural	2nd singular	2nd plural	Imperfect	Pluperfect
a clāmārēmus		✓			✓	
b						
c						
d						
e						
f						
g						
h						

Further work

1 Turn to p. 157, paragraph 6, where you will see the complete imperfect and pluperfect subjunctive tables set out.

How would you recognise the imperfect and pluperfect subjunctive? How would you say they were formed? (If you need help, see pp. 60 and 63.)

Now turn to the imperfect and pluperfect subjunctives of irregular verbs on p. 159. Compare them with the subjunctives of the regular verbs on p. 157. Are they formed in the same way? If you are in any doubt, read again p. 63, paragraph 4 (for the imperfect) and p. 60, paragraph 4 (for the pluperfect).

2 Without looking at the tables, change the following singular forms of the subjunctive to the plural:

audīrēs; portārem; mitteret; mīsisset; timērem;

laudāvissēs; dūxissem; esset.

Check

Word patterns: male and female p. 80

Work through paragraphs 1, 2 and 3.

Further work   **1**   Latin male and female nouns are not always so predictable. For example, what are the Latin nouns for the following roles?

2   English does not generally distinguish male and female by the endings of words, but one common female ending is -ess, e.g. actress. Can you think of other examples with this ending? Think of some of the translations of the female examples in paragraphs 1 and 2.

Check

Practising the language continued p. 81

Ex. 2   Do the exercise as instructed. Then in the table below write down the participle that agrees with the noun, and the case, number and gender of the noun and participle pair.

	Noun	Participle	Case	Number	Gender
a	captīvī				
b	Britannī				
c	ancilla				
d	Cogidubnus				
e	puellam				
f	mīlitēs				

Ex. 3   Do the exercise as instructed. Use the tables on pp. 146–59 to help you if necessary.

Check

The legionary soldier pp. 82–7

Read the text and study the pictures. Then answer the following questions which are based on the pictures as well as the text.

1 **The army as a fighting force**

   a This drawing shows a legionary in battle gear. When facing an enemy force which weapon would he use first? Why?

   b If you were about to engage the legionaries at close quarters, why would they be particularly formidable? See the photograph on p. 85, top right.

2 **The army on parade**

   The photograph on p. 71 shows the army on parade. How many kinds of soldier can you distinguish?

3 **The army at work**

   a What in a legionary's kit would be useful for constructing camps and engineering work?

   b Look at the picture on p. 82. Here the legionaries in the middle of the scene are shown building a bridge with a fort at each end. Towards the right, one legionary hands another a turf, cut to regulation size, while another brings supplies in a basket.

   Can you see what the legionaries have done with their shields and helmets?

   What are the two soldiers on the left doing? (They are not legionaries, but auxiliaries, as is clear from their different clothing and shields.)

4 **The auxiliaries**

   a The auxiliaries provided the army with specialised troops. Can you think of examples in a modern army?

   b The auxiliaries were paid less than the legionaries. What then was the attraction of joining the Roman army?

5 **General question**

   How many reasons can you think of to explain the success of the Roman army? In what situations might it have difficulty?

6 Who was who in the Roman army?

Using the information on p. 86 and the diagram of a legion on p. 87, fill each space below with the most appropriate military title from the box below.

tesserārius	aquilifer	signifer	praefectus castrōrum
lēgātus	cornicen	optiō	centuriō

a _____. Junior officer who organised the guards and received his name from a **tessera**, a small plaque with a password on it.

b _____. One of these in each cohort, who blew the horn to issue commands.

c _____. He was responsible for the training and discipline of a century.

d _____. He bore the silver eagle standard of each legion.

e _____. Each century had one, who carried the standard. He wore a bearskin.

f _____. The highest rank a centurion could attain.

g _____. His name is similar to **legion**, and he was its commander.

h _____. Each centurion had one of these as his deputy.

Check

Vocabulary checklist 25 p. 88

Learn the checklist and answer the following questions.

1 What is an *accident*?

2 What is the *aperture* of a camera?

3 Is a *cogent* argument forceful or weak?

4 If you *confide* in someone, what are you doing?

5 What is an *inexplicable* mistake?

6 How are *extra*-curricular activities different from those on the timetable?

7 If you pay a *nominal* subscription to a club it will be a very small amount. Can you explain the connection between *nominal* and **nōmen**?

8 If you were sent to a *penal* institution, would you be pleased or not? Give your reason.

Check

Language test

1 Select the correct Latin form of the words in **bold type** in the English sentences.

   a **When I was eating** your meal in the kitchen, they were fighting with you. (cum cēnārem, cum cēnāvissem)

   b **When we were soldiers** in Africa, we guarded the whole province. (cum mīlitārēmus, cum mīlitāvissēmus)

   c **When he had shut** the prison door, he asked Modestus where Vercobrix was. (cum clausisset, cum clauderet)

   d **When they had seen** this, they immediately fled. (cum vīdissent, cum vīdērent)

   e **When you were hesitating** outside the cell, Strythio fetched a light. (cum haesitārēs, cum haesitāvissēs)

2 Translate the following sentences.

   a Modestus nesciēbat quō captīvī fūgissent.

   b intellegere nōn poterat cūr Strȳthiō abesset.

   c Modestus eum rogāvit in quā cellā Vercobrix iacēret.

   d nesciēbat cūr Modestus clāmāvisset.

   e Modestum territum rogāvit quid accidisset.

   f centuriō scīre volēbat ubi essēs.

   g Modestus cognōscere nōn potuit quis portam carceris aperuisset.

   h ego optiōnī nārrāvī quō modō tōtam prōvinciam custōdīvissēmus.

 Check

Revision

Participles pp. 161–2

Paras 1–3 Study the sentences, noting again the three different kinds of participles and their meanings.

Para. 4 Translate the sentences and write down the nouns as instructed at the end.

Para. 5 Study the examples.

Further exercise   Complete the following sentences and translate them.

a puellae, in culīnā _____, garriēbant. (labōrāns, labōrantem, labōrantēs)

b soror Vilbiae, fībulam _____, īnspicere volēbat. (cōnspicātus, cōnspicāta, cōnspicātum)

c mīlitēs lēgātum _____ vīdērunt. (appropinquāns, appropinquantem, appropinquantēs)

d Vilbia, ā Modestō _____, thermās intrāvit. (arcessītus, arcessīta, arcessītās)

e centuriō Modestum et Strȳthiōnem, ad castra _____, carcerem custōdīre iussit. (regressum, regressōs, regressī)

Now fill in the table below by writing down the noun and participle pair in each sentence and giving its case, number and gender.

	Noun and participle pair	Case	Number	Gender
a				
b				
c				
d				
e				

Para. 6   Compare the participles with the adjectives on p. 148, as instructed.

Para. 7   First pick out the participle in the sentences and then the noun it agrees with. Think of the case, number and gender of the noun and participle pair and select the correct participle from the tables in paragraph 6.

Irregular verbs pp. 158–9

Revise the forms and tenses of **sum, possum, volō, ferō, eō** and **capiō**.
Work through the examples in paragraph 2 on p. 159 and read paragraph 3.

Further examples   Translate without looking at the tables:

vīs; redībat; cēpistī; tulit; es; nōn poterat; faciunt; velle; fugiēbam; cum abesset.

Check

Progress record Textbook pp. 71–88   Student Study Book pp. 52–66

Stage 25 mīlitēs	Done	Revised	Any problems?
Model sentences			
Strȳthiō			
Modestus custōs			
Practising the language			
About the language 1: indirect questions			
Modestus perfuga I			
Modestus perfuga II			
Modestus perfuga III			
About the language 2: more about the imperfect and pluperfect subjunctive			
Word patterns: male and female			
Practising the language continued			
The legionary soldier			
Vocabulary checklist 25			
Language test			
Revision			

Stage 26 Agricola

Agricola arrives in Chester, where Salvius is anxiously waiting for him.

The fate of Quintus, who is also trying to reach Agricola, is unknown. He has escaped from Belimicus and the horsemen, but is seriously wounded.

Picture p. 89

A triangular terracotta tile from Chester. It was made by the Twentieth Legion (LEGXX) which was stationed in Chester after the Second Legion. The wild boar was the emblem of the Twentieth Legion and the shield with the crossed spears at the top is a victory trophy. This kind of tile was placed along the eaves of buildings to cover the open ends of semi-cylindrical tiles (see picture p. 59).

adventus Agricolae p. 90

Read lines 1–5 and answer the questions.

1   Which legion was based at Chester?

2   **diū et strēnuē** (lines 1–2). Why were the soldiers working like this?

3   **multa et varia faciēbant** (line 4). List the three activities that are mentioned.

Read lines 6–9.

4   Fill in the gaps in this translation.

The soldiers, _____ , were taking the situation badly. They worked for three days on end; _____ Silanus announced the arrival of Agricola. The soldiers, _____ , were extremely pleased because they liked Agricola.

Read lines 10–15 and then answer the questions by translating the Latin given below.

5   Why did Silanus put the soldiers in long rows? *Answer:* **ut Agricolam salūtārent** (lines 10–11).

    It may help to know that **ut** means *so that* or *in order that*.

6   Why did Agricola advance to the platform? *Answer:* **ut pauca dīceret** (line 14).

7   Why did everyone suddenly fall silent? *Answer:* **ut Agricolam audīrent** (lines 14–15).

Read Agricola's speech, lines 16–18.

8 We already know from the story that Agricola was very popular with the soldiers. Say why each of Agricola's three sentences was likely to appeal to the troops.

a gaudeō ... videō. _____

_____

b nūllam ... fortiōrem. _____

_____

c disciplīnam ... laudō. _____

_____

Read lines 19 to the end.

9 Write out a translation. Highlight or underline your translation of **ut eōs īnspiceret** (line 19) and **ut colloquium cum Sīlānō habēret** (line 20).

10 Look back at the sentences containing **ut** that you have just translated.

a Would you say that these sentences tell us:

i the time something happened?

ii the reason something happened?

iii a purpose or intention?

b What do you notice about the verb in the clause that begins with **ut**?

Check

How we know about Agricola p. 91

Read this section, which provides evidence of Agricola's presence in Britain as governor. Later in the Stage you will find out more information about his life which comes from the biography written by his son-in-law, Tacitus.

1 From these inscriptions can you give one way in which the Romans dated their years?

2 Why is it often possible to reconstruct lengthy inscriptions, like the example at the bottom of the page, from just a few groups of letters?

Check

Picture p. 90

Give the rank (and names, if known) of the soldiers in the drawing. Use the text on pp. 90–1 and the pictures on pp. 83, 86 and 87 to help you.

1 _____

2 _____

3 _____

4 _____

5 _____

Check

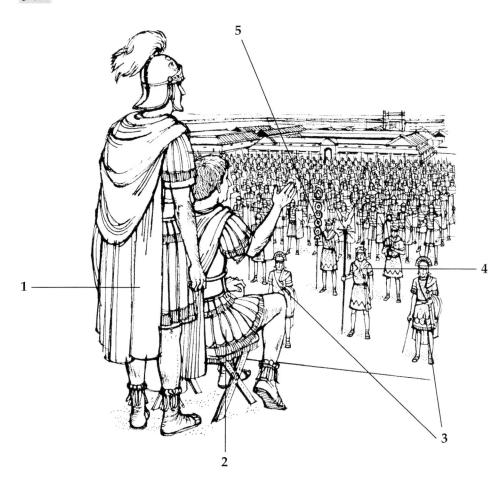

in prīncipiīs pp. 92–3

Lines 1–20 (parāre). Salvius has an interview with Agricola, who takes immediate action as a result.

Read these lines and answer questions 1–7.

Lines 20 (intereā) –33. Salvius introduces Belimicus to support his case, but with unintended results.

Read and answer questions 8–12.

Lines 34 to the end. A sudden arrival brings the story to a dramatic end.

Read and answer questions 13–15.

Further questions

1 Salvius had not originally intended to come north to see Agricola. What had changed his mind?

2 Why was Agricola so upset about Cogidubnus?

3 Did Salvius make the right decision in bringing Belimicus to meet Agricola?

4 Why are Quintus' first words **'cīvis Rōmānus sum'**? Why does he give his full name?

Check

5 The characters below appear in the story. Identify them and choose one adjective from the box to describe each of them, giving a reason for your choice. Choose a different adjective for each character.

| anxious   hasty   efficient   unintelligent   exhausted   brave   shrewd |

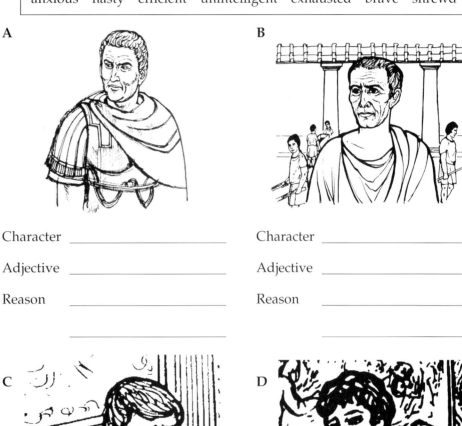

A

Character _____

Adjective _____

Reason _____

_____

B

Character _____

Adjective _____

Reason _____

_____

C

Character _____

Adjective _____

Reason _____

_____

D

Character _____

Adjective _____

Reason _____

_____

Check

About the language 1: purpose clauses p. 94

Para. 1   Read and study the examples and the note. These should be familiar to you from the work you did on the first story, **adventus Agricolae**.

Para. 2   Translate the examples.

Para. 3   Read. You may have already discovered this simpler form of words for yourself. Use this in translating the following sentences taken from **in prīncipiīs**.

    a   subitō Salvius … ad eum festīnāvit ut salūtāret (lines 7–8).

    b   nūper bēstiam in mē impulit ut mē interficeret (lines 28–9).

Check

tribūnus p. 95

Read the following translation of lines 1–6.

When Agricola saw this (i.e. that Quintus had collapsed) *he ordered the guards to remove Quintus and summon a doctor. Then he turned to a tribune of the soldiers, who was standing near.*

'My dear Rufus', he said, 'you are the most intelligent of all the tribunes that I have. I order you to question this man with the greatest care.'

Read lines 7–8.

1   **'omnia explicāre possum'** (line 8). What does this mean? How do you think Salvius said this sentence? Give your reason.

Read lines 9–18.

2   Salvius proceeded to make a series of accusations against Quintus. Which are true (T) and which false (F)? In each case give your reason or comment.

Line	Accusation	T/F	Reason/Comment
9	nūper … nōn invītāveram		
9–10	trēs … dēvorāns		
10–12	duōs … erat		
12–15	ubi … accūsāvit		

3   What was Agricola's reaction to these accusations (line 18)?

Read lines 19 to the end and answer these questions.

4   **'Quīntus Caecilius … est iuvenis summae fideī'** (line 20). How did Rufus' opinion of Quintus differ from that of Salvius: **'multō perfidior est quam Britannī'** (lines 15–16)?

5 What reasons did Rufus have for his opinion of Quintus (lines 20–3)?

6 **patrem meum** (lines 20–1). Do you remember who he was? (If not, see *Book II*, Stages 17–20.)

7 **Salvius ... anxius exiit** (line 25). What reason did Salvius have for being anxious?

8 Which sentence in the story does the picture illustrate? Translate it.

Check

The senior officers in the Roman army p. 100

You have now met Silanus, the commander of the legion, and Rufus, one of the six tribunes in the legion. Read this section and then look back at the diagram on p. 87. You will see that the tribune who came from a noble family was called **tribūnus lāticlāvius**, meaning that he wore a tunic with a broad stripe. Rufus would have been one of the five other tribunes, as he was not of noble birth.

Question   The fact that most senior officers did not stay long in the army could have been disastrous. How did the army still manage to be successful?

Check

About the language 2: gerundives p. 96

Paras 1–2   Latin has several ways of saying that one must or needs to do something. Read paragraphs 1 and 2 to find two ways. In the examples, look carefully at the words which tell us who must do the action:

    mihi   vōbīs   nōbīs   eī

What case is each of these words? (See pp. 152–3, if you are not sure.)

Para. 3   Now complete the translation of the further examples:

a I must _____.

b _____ must walk.

c _____ wait here.

d The slaves _____ work _____.

e All the _____ be silent because the priests are

    _____.

f If they want to see the _____, _____.

Check

contentiō p. 97

Read this translation of lines 1–3 together with the Latin.

When Agricola had listened to Quintus, he furiously summoned Salvius. As soon as he came in, he began to say something. Agricola, however, when he had ordered silence, accused Salvius bitterly.

The rest of the story is mostly taken up with Agricola's accusation of Salvius (lines 4–11) and Salvius' reply (lines 13–19). Choose one of the following options.

Option 1 (lines 4–19) Students working on their own

The speeches of Agricola and Salvius have been summarised below. Write out a translation of each summary and check your work. Then read through the full translation of the speeches which is also provided in the *Answer Key*.

Lines 4–11 *Summary of Agricola's speech*

1 Cogidubnus est innocēns, tū perfidus.

2 amīcī mē dē calliditāte tuā monuērunt.

3 num Imperātor Domitiānus hanc tantam perfidiam ferre potest?

4 in hāc prōvinciā summam potestātem habeō.

5 iubeō tē ad Cogidubnī aulam īre, veniamque ab eō petere.

6 praetereā Imperātōrī ipsī rem explicāre dēbēs.

Lines 13–19 *Summary of Salvius' speech*

1 quam caecus es! quam longē errās!

2 tū victōriās inānēs ē Calēdoniā refers.

3 Imperātor pecūniam opēsque accipere cupit.

4 itaque rēgnum Cogidubnī occupāre cōnstituit.

5 in magnō perīculō es quod cōnsilium meum spernis.

6 nōn sōlum mihi sed Imperātōrī ipsī obstās.

Option 2 (lines 4–19) Students working in groups

Half of you could write out a translation of Agricola's speech in the textbook (lines 4–11) and half of you Salvius' speech (lines 13–19). Then exchange your translations and check each other's work.

Question for everyone (lines 20–2)

What is the unexpected end to this story?

Check

Further work **1** **a** Fill in each of the bubbles with one sentence in Latin, which shows the power that Agricola and Salvius are relying on to win their fight over Cogidubnus. Take the sentences from *either* the summaries in **Option 1** *or* the speeches in the textbook.

b Who will win the power struggle? Give a reason for your opinion.

Check

2 Study again lines 1–2 and the translation:

Agricola, cum Quīntum audīvisset, Salvium furēns arcessīvit. **quī**, simulatque intrāvit, aliquid dīcere coepit.

*When Agricola had listened to Quintus, he furiously summoned Salvius. As soon as **he** came in, he began to say something.*

> Notice that **quī** at the beginning of the second sentence obviously refers to Salvius in the first sentence. It has been translated as *he* and not *who* because this is more idiomatic in English. You could also translate **quī** here as *Salvius*. The relative pronoun **quī** is often used to link sentences together in this way.

Translate the following two sentences into idiomatic English.

Quīntus Rūfō epistulam trādidit. quī, cum eam lēgisset, maximē attonitus erat.

Check

Word patterns: verbs and nouns p. 98

Study paragraphs 1 and 2 and complete the table in paragraph 3.

Further work Some English nouns have the same form and meaning as the Latin nouns, e.g. *tremor* and *terror*.

Work out the identical Latin and English nouns that are connected with the following verbs.

horrēre *to dread;* **errāre** *to make a mistake;* **ardēre** *to be on fire* (literally, or *with love, anger,* etc.); **pallēre** *to be pale*

Check

Practising the language p. 99

Ex. 1 This exercise revises the use of the accusative, genitive and dative cases, singular and plural. Write out as instructed.

Check

If you have selected the wrong choice or the wrong meaning in more than one sentence, check with the tables, pp. 146–7, or **Uses of the cases**, p. 160.

Ex. 2 Write out as instructed and then look again at the sentences.

Which two sentences contain purpose clauses? Which word introduces these?

Sentences   **Introductory word**

Which three sentences contain indirect questions? What are the introductory words for these?

Sentences   **Introductory words**

Ex. 3 Write out as instructed.

Check

Agricola, governor of Britain pp. 100–3

As was mentioned earlier (p. 91) most of what we know about Agricola comes from the biography written by his son-in-law, the historian Tacitus.

1 Read the information. Then study the quotations from Tacitus below and answer the questions, with the help of the information you have read.

   a 'His mother thought it wise to restrain such a passionate interest.'
      What was the 'passionate interest'?

   b 'Neither before nor since has Britain ever been in a more uneasy or dangerous state. Veterans were butchered, towns burnt to the ground, armies isolated.'
      What dangerous situation in Agricola's earlier career is referred to here?

   c 'Our national dress came into favour and the toga was everywhere to be seen.'
      Why do you think Agricola encouraged this development?

   d 'With an army marching light…(Agricola) reached Mons Graupius, which he found occupied by the enemy.'
      Where was Mons Graupius? What happened there?

2 Why was Agricola not typical of the senior officers in the Roman army?

Check

Pictures

p. 101   Antefix. See this book p. 68 for an explanation.

The boar's-head trumpet. The sound came out at the boar's mouth on the left; the rest of the trumpet was broken off at the neck.

p. 102   The camp at Chew Green. For the rough location of this camp, turn to p. 139. Chew Green was on Dere Street north of Corstopitum, modern Corbridge.

p. 103   What do you think the effect of this sculpture would have been on the Caledonians?

Check

Vocabulary checklist 26 p. 104

Learn the checklist and answer the following questions.

1   A *belligerent* person is someone who

   a   is beautiful

   b   behaves aggressively

   c   has a large stomach.

2   People who are excited or upset sometimes cause a _____.

3   A *docile* dog is not likely to run wild. Explain the link with **docēre**.

4   Why are some dogs called *Fido*?

5   The rail company set a _____ of how many children could travel free of charge.

Using the Latin words as clues, replace the English word in *italic type* with another of the same meaning.

6   The athlete's *most far-reaching* ambition was to win an Olympic gold medal (**ultimus**).

7   The *next-to-last* page of the book has been cut out (**paene ultimus**).

8   I was *directed* to the library for more information (**referre**).

9   He enjoyed *telling* the story to his grandchildren (**referre**). Clue: Look at the fourth part of the verb.

10   Translate: abstulī; abstuleram; īnstruunt; īnstrūxērunt; praebēbāmus; praebuistī.

Check

Language test

1 Translate the following sentences, highlighting or underlining the purpose clause in the Latin and your translation:

   a lēgātus mīlitēs īnstrūxit ut Agricola eōs īnspiceret.

   b Agricola Quīntum ad sē vocāvit ut colloquium habēret.

   c omnia Agricolae nārrāvī ut mihi crēderet.

   d mīles ad castra festīnāvit ut mortem Cogidubnī nūntiāret.

   e diū manēbāmus ut vērum cognōscerēmus.

   f mē vīsitāvistī ut pecūniam meam auferrēs.

2 Translate the following sentences:

   a mīlitibus festīnandum est.

   b captīvīs nōn effugiendum est.

   c vōbīs quam celerrimē currendum est.

   d custōdibus in carcere nōn dormiendum est.

   e sī Imperātor adest, omnibus tacendum est.

Revision

ipse p. 154

You have now met **ipse** several times in *Books II* and *III*. Study the translated examples and note that **ipse** emphasises the word it describes. In the first example **ipsa** means *herself* because it describes **domina** (which is feminine); in the second, it means *himself*, because **ipsīus** describes **Imperātōris** (which is masculine).

Now study the table. You will find the forms are like those of **bonus** (p. 148) except for the nominative masculine singular, and the genitive and dative singular. Do the genitive and dative singular remind you of other pronouns you have met?

Translate the further examples.

Word order p. 165

Paras 1–3 Study the different word orders in these paragraphs and translate the further examples in your head.

Para. 4 Write out a translation of the examples. Look at the Latin again. Where do all the verbs come in the sentences? The position of the nominative varies: where does it come in each sentence?

Why does the order of words in a Latin sentence vary, and yet the sentence still makes sense?

Para. 5 Read and translate the examples in your head.

Check

More about word order

As you have seen from *Book I* onwards, there are many different word orders in Latin. If you look at the sentences you have just translated, they all make sense because the endings of the words tell you what part they are playing in the sentence.

In English we depend on a much more fixed order of words to convey the meaning. For example, we have to translate **poposcit captīvus aquam** (paragraph **4d**) as *The prisoner demanded water* because any other word order would be nonsensical, e.g. *He demanded the prisoner water*. But Latin can have

1   captīvus aquam poposcit

2   aquam poposcit captīvus

3   poposcit aquam captīvus

4   poposcit captīvus aquam

and the sentences all make sense.

In Latin, as you already know, the most usual word order is NOMINATIVE + ACCUSATIVE + VERB, as in sentence **1** above: **captīvus aquam poposcit**. If the order is changed as in sentence **2**, the sentence still means *The prisoner demanded water*, but by putting **aquam** as first word, we give it more emphasis: ***It was water** the prisoner demanded*.

The last word in a Latin sentence is often emphatic, too. You will find that a writer keeps you in suspense waiting for the last word. For example, when Quintus makes his dramatic entrance into the headquarters at Chester, the writer uses this word order: **per iānuam prīncipiōrum perrūpit homō squālidus** (p. 92, lines 34–5).

We have to wait until the last two words to know who it was that burst through the door of the headquarters: it was a *man* and he was *covered in filth*.

English can occasionally create this kind of suspense: *Through the door of the headquarters burst a man covered in filth*.

To sum up: Latin often gives special emphasis to a word by placing it first or last in a sentence.

Translate the following sentences. Which Latin word is emphasised the most? What effect do you think is intended?

1   cum Modestus in cellā stāret, in eum incidit arānea.

2   optima ōmina nōbīs dea mīsit.

Check

Pronouns III: quī p. 155

Para. 1 You are already familiar with the nominative and accusative of **quī**. Now the genitive and dative forms are added to the table. Compare these forms with those of **ipse** and the other pronouns on pp. 153–4. What conclusions do you draw?

Study the examples which are translated for you and then write out a translation of the further examples. Pick out the relative pronoun in each sentence and the noun it describes (i.e. its antecedent) and work out the case, number and gender of the pronoun. Then complete the following table.

Noun	Relative pronoun	Case of relative pronoun	Number of relative pronoun	Gender of relative pronoun
a				
b				
c				
d				
e				
f				

Para. 2 This will be studied in Stage 28, when you have met more examples.

Check

Progress record Textbook pp. 89–104 Student Study Book pp. 68–80

Stage 26 Agricola	Done	Revised	Any problems?
adventus Agricolae			
How we know about Agricola			
in prīncipiīs			
About the language 1: purpose clauses			
tribūnus			
The senior officers in the Roman army			
About the language 2: gerundives			
contentiō			
Word patterns: verbs and nouns			
Practising the language			
Agricola, governor of Britain			
Vocabulary checklist 26			
Language test			
Revision			

Stage 27 in castrīs

We now meet Modestus and Strythio again after the disaster in Stage 25 when Vercobrix, son of the Celtic chief, escaped while in their custody.

The picture shows them deciding where to hide. Modestus is pointing to a granary, which is where the events of this Stage take place.

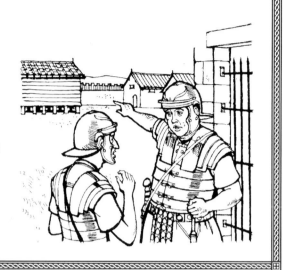

Picture p. 105

This is a model of the legionary fortress at Deva (Chester). It was ideally situated near the river so provisions could reach the camp easily and there was easy access to the sea. Notice its standard 'playing-card' shape, with four main gates. There is a detailed plan of a legionary fortress on p. 115.

The streets and walls of present-day Chester still follow to some extent those of the Roman fortress, and the foundations of many buildings have been excavated in the cellars of shops.

Model sentences p. 106

Read the sentences and study the pictures to guide you to the meaning. Then answer the following questions and complete the translations.

imperābat: imperāre	*order*

Sentences 1 a **'fuge mēcum ad horreum!'** What did Modestus say to Strythio?

b Which word tells you how the pair were feeling?

c Fill in the missing words. Modestus was advising Strythio

_____.

Sentences 2 a What did the centurion actually say?

b **prō prīncipiīs.** Where was the centurion giving his orders?

c The centurion was ordering the soldiers _____

_____.

Sentences 3 a What did Vercobrix actually say?

   b Where was Vercobrix making his speech?

   c Vercobrix was urging the Britons _____

   _____.

Further questions 1 Read p. 106 again and write down the meaning of these three verbs.

   monēre   _____

   imperāre   _____

   incitāre   _____

   In the model sentences, which word follows each one of these verbs? _____

   2 What differences do you see between the Roman and British troops in the last two pictures?

   Check

Granaries

   1 Study the picture of the reconstruction of a wooden granary on p. 107. How was the floor kept free from damp and air allowed to circulate?

   2 a Read about granaries on p. 117. Later ones were made of stone, but the means of keeping grain dry were similar. How did the roof design also help?

   b How much grain could granaries in a fortress store?

   Check

in horreō p. 107

   Modestus and Strythio escape to a granary, where they find a hole in one of the walls. Read this translation of lines 1–8 along with the Latin.

   Modestus and Strythio, having left the prison, fled to a granary. They crawled through a narrow opening and stayed hidden in the granary. The centurion, when he had seen the gates of the cells open and the prison deserted, was very angry. He ordered the soldiers to capture Modestus and Strythio. The soldiers, however, although they searched through the whole camp, could not find them. They stayed hidden for two days. On the third day Modestus was so miserable that he could not bear the situation any longer.

   Read lines 9–16 and answer the questions.

   1 Find three expressions which show that Modestus is depressed (lines 9–12).

   2 'frūmentum ... cōnsūmere nōn possum' (lines 10–11). Why not?

   3 What does Strythio offer to do (lines 14–15)?

   4 Why does he think this will cheer up Modestus?

Read lines 17–26 and answer the questions.

5 **'nōbīs cēnandum est'** (line 17). Translate this sentence.

6 Modestus suggests four things to improve the situation and four people to provide them. Match the objects in the pictures below with the people.

Aulus ___   coquus ___   Nigrina ___   Publicus ___

A

B

C

D

Read lines 27 to the end, and then answer the questions.

7 Who can't be persuaded to come to the party?

8 Can you suggest a reason?

Check

About the language 1: indirect commands pp. 108–9

Paras 1 and 2 Read these paragraphs, which show you how direct commands can be reported as indirect commands.

Para. 3 Study the examples. Remind yourself of these examples from **in horreō** and complete the translations. Then write down in English the direct command.

    a centuriō mīlitibus imperāvit ut Modestum et Strȳthiōnem caperent.

    The centurion ordered the soldiers _____.

    Direct command: ____ _____

    b Strȳthiō coquō persuāsit ut cēnam splendidam parāret.

    Strythio persuaded the cook _____.

    Direct command: _____

    c Nigrīnam ōrāvit ut in castra venīret.

    He begged Nigrina _____.

    Direct command: _____

Para. 4 Translate the further examples.

Check

Modestus prōmōtus I pp. 109–10

Modestus, while waiting in the dark for
his friends, gets a nasty surprise.

Read lines 1–11 and fill in the gaps in the translation.

When Strythio _____ dinner and his friends, ten Britons, _____

_____, were cautiously approaching the camp. For Vercobrix _____

_____ to attack the camp. After the Britons avoided the guards,

they _____. They were holding torches in their hands ____

_____. They reached the

granaries quickly because earlier _____ where _____.

Modestus, _____, was sitting in the granary. He

was so hungry _____. He was looking out through

the opening, _____. 'I've already been

waiting for _____. What _____?'

Suddenly _____ a band of men _____.

Read lines 12–24 and translate them in your head. Then study the summary of
events below. Choose the correct nouns to complete each sentence.

Britannī	Modestus (use twice)
Vercobrix	Britannus quīdam

1 _____ called out 'Friends, come over here!'

2 _____, in amazement, didn't dare to reply.

3 _____ made an insulting remark about Modestus and said he was
harmless.

4 _____ bumped into Modestus and was mistaken for Nigrina.

5 _____ asked who had the lamp.

Translate lines 25 to the end.

Check

Further work 1 Pick out and write down two indirect commands in this story. One is between
lines 1 and 7, the other between lines 25 and 29. Remember you are looking
for someone telling or persuading someone to do something.

2 Look at **in manibus facēs tenēbant** (lines 4–5) and **manum hominum …
cōnspexit** (line 11).
   The word **manus** has different meanings in these sentences. What are the
meanings?

Check

Modestus prōmōtus II pp. 110–11

Read lines 1–15 and answer questions 1–7 on p. 111. Before you begin, a reminder: **tantus** means *so great*, **adeō** *so greatly, so much*.

Read lines 16 to the end, and then *either* answer questions 8–12 *or* mark T (True) or F (False) by the following statements; if you decide a statement is false, give your reason.

Statement	T/F	Reason if false
1 Modestus prepared an ambush for the Britons.		
2 There was a brief struggle.		
3 Modestus and his friends easily overpowered the Britons.		
4 Then Modestus summoned the commander.		
5 Modestus was so pleased that he could hardly contain himself.		
6 Modestus was delighted when he received money as a reward.		

Check

About the language 2: result clauses p. 112

Para. 1 Study the examples. Then read these sentences taken from recent stories and complete the translations.

1 Modestus adeō ēsuriēbat ut dē vītā paene dēspērāret.

Modestus was so hungry _____

_____ .

2 Britannī erant tam attonitī ut immōtī stārent.

The Britons were so astonished _____

_____ .

3 tantī erant clāmōrēs Modestī ut tōta castra complērent.

So great were the shouts of Modestus _____

_____ .

4 tantus erat numerus mīlitum ut Britannōs facile superārent.

So great was the number of the soldiers _____

_____ .

Para. 2   Translate the further examples.

Para. 3   Read the note about result clauses and then complete the table below by adding the signal words and meanings from the last three sentences in paragraph 2.

Signal word	Meaning
tantus	*so great*

Check

The legionary fortress   pp. 115–19

Study the text and pictures and then answer the following questions.

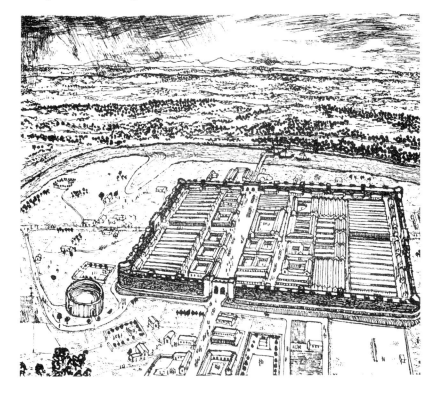

1   This is a drawing of the fortress at Chester based on the panoramic view on p. 105. Indicate on the drawing with the appropriate letters:

   A Any part of the fortress where Modestus and Strythio might have lived.

   B The building where they would have been tried if their misdeeds in the prison had come to light.

   C The area where Nigrina lived.

   D The place where official entertainments were laid on for the soldiers.

2 Can you sort out these muddled pairs by putting the letters on the left next to the correct descriptions? The first one is done for you.

	Latin word	Letter	Description
a	horreum		hospital
b	prīncipia		pair of rooms for eight men
c	sacellum		civilian settlement
d	contubernium	a	granary
e	praetōrium		headquarters building
f	vīcus		house of commanding officer
g	valētūdinārium		shrine

3 Consider these questions. You need not write out the answers, and if you have a partner or are in a group, you could discuss them together.

   a Why could a soldier, recently arrived from Germany, find his way around the fortress at Chester without any difficulty?

   b At the time of these stories, a century contained 80 men. What do you think its original number was?

   c Look at the picture on p. 96. Smoke is rising from the ovens, placed next to the rampart. Why did the Romans put the ovens here and not in the middle of the barrack blocks?

   d Why did the Romans site the principia towards the centre of the fortress instead of just inside the main gate?

Check

Word patterns: adjectives and nouns p. 113

Work your way through paragraphs 1–5 as instructed.

Check

Practising the language p. 114

Ex. 1   Write out this exercise as instructed.

Check

If you have made more than three mistakes, read the language note on p. 161.

Ex. 2   This exercise is quite difficult and, if possible, you may like to work with a partner. Do sentences **a**, **c**, **e**, **f** and **g** as instructed and then check your answers. If you have got them all right or made only one mistake, you need only write down the required Latin word in the remaining examples. Otherwise write out the rest of the examples as before.

Check

Ex. 3   Work in the same way as with exercise 2, doing **a–f** first.

Check

Further work   Be careful in identifying the genitive plural forms of third declension nouns. Look again at exercise 3, sentence **h**, and then study the genitive plural ending of the nouns in the table on p. 147.

Translate these examples:

manus mīlitum

a band _____

Nigrīna, optima saltātrīcum

Nigrina, the best _____

magnus numerus nāvium

a great number _____

Check

Vocabulary checklist 27   p. 120

Learn the checklist and answer the following questions.

1   'His *apparent* reason for leaving was his wish to spend more time with his family.' What does *apparent* mean?

2   What would you have done if you have been found guilty of *arson*?

3   How would you behave if you adopted an *imperious* tone of voice?

4   What is an *incendiary* bomb designed to do?

5   'The patient's disease was *insidious*.' Was the disease easily spotted? What is the connection with **īnsidiae**?

6   A *manual* could also be called a _____book.

7   'Its *proximity* to bus and train routes makes the shopping centre popular.' Explain.

8   '*Quality*, not quantity, is what counts in writing essays.' What does this mean?

9   Would you be safe in a house where the electrical wiring was *sub-standard*?

10   A *tacit* agreement involves no discussion. Why not?

Check

Language test

1   Translate the following sentences and give the case and number of the words in **bold type**.

a   Agricola, valdē commōtus, **iussum** lēgātō dedit.

b   ingēns multitūdō **cīvium** senātōrem in forō circumvēnit.

c   **praemium**, quod Modestus accēperat, eum nōn dēlectāvit.

d   Quīntus et Dumnorix magnam **manum equitum** appropinquantem cōnspexērunt.

2 Complete the sentences with clauses chosen from the box below. Then translate the sentences.

> ut eās numerāre nōn posset
> ut ante noctem domum redīrem
> ut fīlium servāret
> ut dē vītā dēspērārēmus
> ut ad prīncipia contenderētis
> ut respondēre nōn audērent

a fēmina mīlitem ōrāvit _____.

b mercātor tot gemmās habēbat _____.

c puerī adeō timēbant _____.

d pater meus saepe mē monēbat _____.

e tantum erat perīculum _____.

f centuriō vōbīs imperāvit _____.

3 Translate the following sentences and give the tense and person of each verb. For example:

> quandō ad Britanniam **vēnistis**?
> *When did you come to Britain?*
> **vēnistis**: 2nd person plural, perfect tense.

a ēheu! domus tua **ardet**!

b maximē **gaudēbam** quod dea precēs meās **audīverat**.

c cūr fīliīs adeō **nocuistī** ut tē vīsitāre **recūsārent**?

d cum Modestus haec verba **dīxisset**, eī nōn **crēdidimus**.

Check

Revision

Uses of the subjunctive p. 163

Read paragraphs 1, 2 and 3 and do the further examples.

Check

Longer sentences pp. 166–7

Study paragraph 1 and then translate all three sentences in paragraph 2a.

Check

If you have got these right, do examples **b** and **c**, translating the third sentence only in each example. If you had problems with example **a**, translate all the sentences in **b** and **c**.

Para. 3   Translate the examples.

Check

Progress record Textbook pp. 105–20 Student Study Book pp. 82–90

Stage 27 in castrīs	Done	Revised	Any problems?
Model sentences			
Granaries			
in horreō			
About the language 1: indirect commands			
Modestus prōmōtus I			
Modestus prōmōtus II			
About the language 2: result clauses			
The legionary fortress			
Word patterns: adjectives and nouns			
Practising the language			
Vocabulary checklist 27			
Language test			
Revision			

Stage 28 imperium

After the death of Cogidubnus, Salvius takes over his kingdom and brutally puts down any Britons who resist his demands for money.

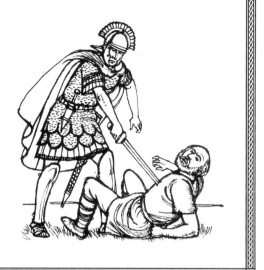

Picture p. 121

This large cameo, 22 cm in diameter, shows the eagle, a symbol of Jupiter, king of the gods, and also the symbol of Roman power. It stands on a palm branch, symbol of victory, and grips a wreath of oak leaves, a decoration given to those who had saved the life of a fellow-citizen. The cameo was made for the Emperor Augustus to celebrate his coming to power in 27 BC.

A cameo is a stone or shell with two layers of colours; the upper layer is carved with a scene or figure (here the eagle) which stands out from the lower layer, which forms the background. This cameo is made from onyx. The circular frame was added in the 16th century.

Model sentences pp. 122–4

Read the introduction at the top of page 122 and answer the following questions.

extorquēre	*extort, force*
dīripere	*ransack*

1 Which two things did Salvius do after the death of Cogidubnus?

2 What resistance did he meet?

3 What was Salvius' reaction?

4 Translate these two sentences:

    a Salvium adiuvābat Belimicus, prīnceps Canticōrum.

    b centuriōnem mīlitibus praefēcit.

pp. 122–3   Study the pictures and sentences and then answer the questions below.

armātī: armāre	*arm*
spē: spēs	*hope*

Sentence 1   **a**   What did the soldiers do?

               b   How were they armed?

Sentence 2   Fill in the gaps in this translation.

               The farmer, wounded _____ of the centurion, fell down unconscious.

Sentence 3   **clāmōribus territī**. How are the slaves described?

Sentence 4   **fūste armātus**. How was the farmer's son armed? Explain why his resistance was in vain.

Sentence 5   Belimicus was helping and encouraging the Roman soldiers. **spē praemiī adductus** explains why he was motivated to do this. Can you translate the phrase?

Sentence 6   Why are the soldiers finding it difficult to carry away the chest?

Check

p. 124   Study the pictures and sentences. Then fill in the missing words in these translations.

catēnīs: catēna	*chain*
vīnctās: vincīre	*bind*
ventō: ventus	*wind*
auctae: augēre	*increase*
īrā: īra	*anger*

Sentence 7   *Then the soldiers led the women, _____, to the camp.*

Sentences 8   *The flames, _____, quickly consumed the cottage.*

Sentences 9   Translate.

Check

testāmentum   p. 125

The will of Cogidubnus, like other Roman wills and most modern ones, is a formal document, which uses legal language and full names to prevent misunderstandings. This will can be divided into three parts:

     the naming of the heir

     various bequests

     funeral arrangements and the safe-keeping of the will.

     Read lines 1–6 and answer the questions.

1   What Latin phrase suggests that Cogidubnus made his will shortly before his death? Translate the phrase.

2   Whom does Cogidubnus name as his heir? What does he leave him?

3   What order does he give the Regnenses?

Lines 7–20 list the bequests or legacies. Note that each starts with the standard legal phrase **dō lēgō** I give I bequeath, followed by the full name of the beneficiary, i.e. the person receiving the bequest.

4   Fill in the following table with the bequests made to the various beneficiaries and the reason why they were made.

Beneficiary	Bequest	Reason for bequest
Cn. Iūlius Agricola		
C. Salvius Līberālis		
L. Marcius Memor		
Dumnorix		
Belimicus		

Finally (lines 21 to the end), Cogidubnus gives directions about his funeral and the safe-keeping of his will.

5   Who is to carry out Cogidubnus' funeral instructions? Why do you think he gives these instructions?

6   What is to be buried with Cogidubnus? Do the contents of his grave remind you of anything you have seen in excavations or in museums?

7   **manū meā scrīptum ānulōque meō signātum** (lines 25–6). Why do you think these phrases are included in the will?

8   Look through the will again. Which parts strike you as unexpected or surprising? Have you any explanation?

Check

Picture p. 125

What building is shown in the picture? Why do you think Salvius' portrait is superimposed on it?

Check

in aulā Salviī pp. 126–7

Salvius proceeds to the palace. He soon learns that Belimicus is plotting against him.

Read lines 1–14 and answer questions 1–7. If you are in a group you could do this in pairs and then compare answers.

Check

Read lines 15 to the end and answer questions 8–12 on your own.

Check

Further work

1 Translate the following phrases and answer the questions. You may need to go back to the story to answer some of them.

    a **nōnnūllī prīncipēs, avāritiā et metū corruptī** (line 5). What does this tell you about these chieftains? About Salvius?

    b **(Belimicus), hāc spē adductus** (line 9). What was Belimicus' hope?

    c **Salvius, audāciā Belimicī incēnsus** (line 12). Why was Salvius so angry with Belimicus?

    d **venēnum cibō mixtum** (line 20). Who suggested this?

    e **Salvius, cōnsiliō amīcī dēlectātus** (line 22). Why was the plan so agreeable to Salvius?

    f **quī, epistulā mendācī dēceptus** (lines 26–7). What was in the letter?

2 Translate the following pairs of sentences which are shortened versions of those in the story. You will probably translate **quī** at the beginning of the second sentence in each pair as *who*. Can you think of a better English translation?

    a Belimicus cum paucīs prīncipibus coniūrāre coepit. **quī**, tamen, rem Salviō rettulērunt.

    b Salvius Belimicum ad aulam invītāvit. **quī** ad aulam nōnā hōrā vēnit.

    How did you translate **quī** in question 1f above?

    Now turn to p. 155, paragraph 2, which explains this particular use of the relative pronoun, and translate the further examples at the bottom of the page.

About the language 1: the ablative case p. 128

Para. 1 Study the sentences and their translations. How is the ablative case, printed in **bold type**, translated in these sentences?

    You will be pleased that the ablative is the last case of the noun that you will learn.

Para. 2 Study the endings of the nominative and ablative cases in the first, second and third declensions. You will notice that some of the ablative endings are the same as those of other cases. For example, in the plural the ablatives are exactly the same as the dative plural. As usual, the sense of the sentence will make the meaning clear.

Para. 3 Translate the further examples. Pick out the ablative case in each sentence and say whether it is singular or plural.

Add the missing cases to the table below. To do this you may need to consult the table in paragraph 2 and the **Vocabulary** at the end of the book.

	nominative singular	ablative singular	ablative plural
first declension	. . . .	iniūriā	. . . .
	. . . .	. . . .	catēnīs
second declension	. . . .	gladiō	. . . .
third declension	. . . .	. . . .	clāmōribus

Check

cēna Salviī p. 129

Fill in the gaps in the following translation of lines 1–11.

Salvius received Belimicus kindly _____ *and led him into the*

dining-room. There _____ *lavishly and in high spirits. Belimicus,*

_____ *and relaxed by the wine,* _____

_____ *boldly:*

'My dear Salvius, _____ *many great acts of kindness from me.*

After _____, *I alone helped you; having*

pursued them _____, _____ *Dumnorix;* _____

many lies _____

Cogidubnus for treachery. For such great favours as these _____ *a*

well-deserved reward.'

When Salvius heard this, _____, *he*

however concealed his anger and answered _____.

Now read the rest of the story and answer these questions.

1 How did Salvius reassure Belimicus about his reward (line 12)?
2 How did Salvius pretend that he was an attentive and generous host (lines 12–14)?
3 Do you think the sauce had already been poisoned? Give a reason (line 15).
4 What did Salvius ask Belimicus (lines 17–18)?
5 What was Belimicus' reply? Do you think Salvius was expecting it?
6 What did Salvius tell Belimicus about the **aureī** (lines 21–2)?

7 **illud testāmentum ... ego scrīpsī** (lines 24–5). Why did Salvius feel safe in making this confession? How do you think Belimicus will react?

8

Look at the picture. What point in the story does it refer to?

Further work   Look again at the following words in lines 1–11:

> **benignē** (line 1); **sūmptuōsē** and **hilarē** (line 2); **audācter** (line 4);
> **cōmiter** (line 11).

Can you remember what these words ending in **-ē** and **-ter** are called? If in doubt, look at **Word patterns** on pp. 12 and 32.

Check

About the language 2: expressions of time   p. 130

You have met several examples of these already and will have translated them correctly because the context of the sentence makes the meaning obvious.

Study paragraphs 1 and 2 and then translate the examples in paragraph 3. Pick out all the expressions of time and say whether they are accusative or ablative.

Check

Picture   p. 130

Originally this amphora, like many others, would have had a spike at the bottom. The contents of an amphora are often identified by the shape or the writing on the stopper or on the jar itself. Do you remember what kind of sauce garum was?

Belimicus rēx   p. 131

In this final story in *Book III* Salvius promises to make Belimicus a king, as he desires. But his kingdom is to be very different from the one he is expecting.

Read lines 1–11 and answer the questions.

1   Why was Belimicus **attonitus** (line 1)? How did he show this?

2   **rīdēns** (line 2). Why do you think Salvius laughed at Belimicus' astonishment? According to Salvius, why had Belimicus no hope of receiving anything from Cogidubnus (lines 3–4)?

3 What did Salvius say about his own relationship with Belimicus?

4 Study the following sentences (lines 5–7) in turn. Explain why Belimicus would become more and more pleased as he heard each sentence.

    a tibi multum dēbeō, ut dīxistī.

       ut here means *as*.

    b itaque rēgem tē creāre in animō habeō.

    c sed rēgnum quod tibi dēstinō multō maius est quam Cogidubnī.

5 **heus! ... effūdit** (lines 7–10). Describe how the poison came to be administered.

6 **ignārus perīculī mortis** (line 11). Why was Belimicus unaware of the danger?

Read lines 12–21. Belimicus' words are translated for you. Fill in Salvius' responses to him.

    Belimicus: *How big is this kingdom which you have promised me? Where in the world is it?*

    Salvius: (laughing loudly) _____

    Belimicus: (alarmed by these words) *You have drunk too much, my friend. I know of no kingdom greater than the Roman empire.*

    Salvius: _____

    _____

    _____

    _____

Check

Filming notes Translate lines 22 to the end in your head. Then imagine that you are filming this scene. Make notes for yourself under the following headings:

Belimicus (lines 22–6)

State of mind _____

Physical symptoms _____

_____

Tone of speech _____

Salvius (lines 27–9)

Contrast with Belimicus: appearance / tone of speech _____

_____

Death of Belimicus (lines 30–1) _____

_____

Disposal of body (lines 31–3)

Change of tempo _____

_____

Cremation: pyre previously prepared?

_____

_____

_____

_____

End of scene (**sīc Salvius … manērent** lines 33–4)
How to convey visually / with speech? _____

_____

_____

Check

About the language 3: prepositions pp. 132–3

Study paragraphs 1–3. Most of the prepositions will be very familiar to you. This language note explains that some are followed by the accusative and some by the ablative.

Translate the examples in paragraph 4.

Further work Compile a table that you can keep for reference. Copy down the headings in the table below.

Look again at the sentences in paragraph 4 and your translation. Enter the prepositions and their nouns, and the translation, in the table. The first three examples are done for you.

Prepositions

Accusative	Translation	Ablative	Translation
ad urbem	to the city	dē morte	about the death
prope templum	near the temple		

If you do not know the meaning of a preposition or which column to put it in, you will find the answer in paragraphs 2 and 3.

Now translate the following phrases and add them to the correct column, again using paragraphs 2 and 3 to help you.

> ante bellum, ā silvā, trāns flūmen, extrā mūrōs, cum amīcīs, ē fonte, post cēnam, per hostēs.

Read paragraph 5 and translate the examples in your head. Add to your table examples of **in** with the accusative and **in** with the ablative and translate them.

Look again at your table. Is there any way of knowing which prepositions are used with an accusative and which with an ablative?

Answer: Prepositions that denote movement *towards, against* or *through* are used with the *accusative*; those that denote movement *out of* or *from* with the *ablative*. The cases used with other prepositions are not so obvious but these phrases are easy to translate, as you have found since the beginning of the Course.

Check

Interpreting the evidence: our knowledge of Roman Britain pp. 135–9

Read the introduction.

Literary evidence p. 135

Read and then study the following:

In his biography of his father-in-law, Agricola, Tacitus gives the speech made by Agricola to his troops before the battle against the Scots at **mōns Graupius** (see the map on p. 139). Here are some extracts from it.

> *'For seven years, my fellow soldiers, you have been conquering Britain by the might and divine guidance of Rome and by our own loyal endeavours. In so many campaigns, in so many battles – whether we have needed courage in the face of the enemy or endurance and toil against nature herself – I have never been ashamed of my soldiers nor you of your leader. And so we have passed beyond the limits reached by former governors and earlier armies and we hold the furthest part of Britain, not by unconfirmed reports or rumour, but with fortresses and arms. ...*
>
> *'The fiercest of the Britons have long since fallen; what remains is a cowardly and frightened rabble. Now you have at last found them; but they did not mean to resist – they have been trapped. Their desperate situation and the paralysis resulting from their extreme fear have fixed them on this spot where you may win a fine and splendid victory. Finish with campaigning; crown fifty years of fighting with a famous day; and prove to our country that her army could never be blamed for prolonging or renewing the war.'*

Now answer the following questions.

1 What do you think would be the effect of the speech on the soldiers?

2 What would be the effect of the speech on the Romans who read the book?

3 How might Tacitus have known what was said?

4 What do you think was his aim in including this speech?

Archaeological evidence pp. 136–9

Read this section and study the pictures.

1 The two pictures on p. 136 show rescue excavations. What does this mean?

2 Look at the diagram on p. 137. When the archaeologists were excavating Fishbourne why would they be taking frequent photographs and making drawings of the different layers? Use the information in paragraph 2, p. 136 to help you.

3 Study the two pictures at the bottom of p. 137. Which one shows the earlier stage of the excavation? Do the post holes in the right-hand picture remind you of a planting scheme at Fishbourne?

4 You have already seen the objects below, which were excavated in Roman Britain. What information might they give to archaeologists?

A

from Chester

B

from Fishbourne

C

from East Anglia

5 In this copy of the plan of Silchester, can you mark in

the forum
the amphitheatre
the defensive ditch outside the town?

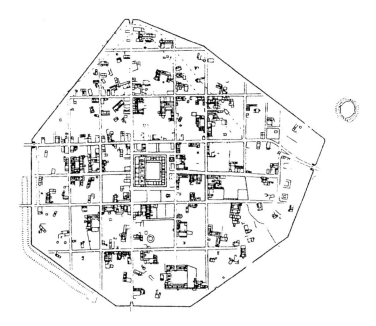

6 Why does the pattern of streets mark Silchester out as a town laid out by the Romans?

7 Study the map on p. 139. Can you find the Roman names for the following towns and cities?

London	St Albans
Bath	Carlisle
Chester	Corbridge
Silchester	Caerleon
Chichester	Wroxeter
York	Exeter
Gloucester	Lincoln
Colchester	Cirencester

8 Notice in the list above the name *Chester* and other names of towns that end in *-chester* and *-xeter*. They are all derived from **castra**, a word which was known to the Anglo-Saxons and which they used to name settlements that grew up in or near ex-Roman camps or towns. The Welsh equivalent is *caer* as in *Caerleon*.

Can you think of other towns whose names are derived from **castra**?

Check

Word patterns: adjectives and nouns p. 133

Study the examples in paragraph 1 and then do the exercises in paragraphs 2 and 3 as instructed.

Look at all the nouns. As a group their meanings have something in common. Can you say what it is?

Check

Practising the language p. 134

Ex. 1   Do the exercise as instructed.

Further work   Write down why the subjunctive is being used in each sentence.

Ex. 2   Do the exercise as instructed.
Check

Interpreting the evidence continued

Inscriptional evidence pp. 140–1

Read the introduction. The easiest way to cope with reading the inscription at the top of the page is to cover up the explanations in yellow and uncover them one by one as you go through the inscription line by line. You can see the expanded version on the opposite page, with a translation.

Using this inscription as a model and referring to the notes, see how much of the other inscriptions on p. 141 you can decipher.

The five points asked for on p. 141 should be quite easy to find; see the *Answer Key* for the rest of the information. In both inscriptions you will find that some letters have been run together, e.g. A and E in CAECILIVS and A and V in AVITVS. Note that the letter V is used for both V and U in inscriptions, as in the names 'Caecilius' and 'Avitus'.

Check

Vocabulary checklist 28 p. 142

Learn the checklist and answer the following questions.

1   A *corps de ballet* will never be composed of *corpulent* members. Why not? What is the connection of these words with **corpus**?

2   He was *irascible* by nature, but was not *irate* when the puppy chewed his slippers. What is the difference between these two words?

3   The defendant was accused of acting with *malice aforethought*. What is meant by this? Which word is derived from Latin?

4   The house was furnished in a most *opulent* style. What impression did its owner intend to convey?

5   What is the connection between **spēs**, **spērāre** and **dēspērāre**?

6 Give the different meanings of **ut** in these two sentences:

amīcus meus laetissimus erat, ut vīdī.

amīcus meus mē in hortum dūxit ut flōrēs vidērem.

7 What is the purpose of a *ventilator*?

8 Translate the following: cōnstituere; dolēbātis; mandāveram; occīdērunt.

Numbers 1 Explain the meaning of the following: ***unicycle, duet, trident, quatrain, quinquereme, sextet, septuagenarian, octave, November, decimal.***

2 What do the Latin numbers for 30, 40, ..., 90 have in common?

3 Is there more liquid in a *centilitre* or a *millilitre*?

Check

Language test

1 Use the words in the box to translate the phrases in *italic type* in the sentences below. All the words must be used. You will also need to use some of the numbers that occur in the checklist for this Stage.

annō	annōs	prīmō
hōrā	hōrās	secundō
diē	diēs	tertiā
nocte	noctēs	illā

a We lived in Rome *for six years*.

b The prisoner refused food *for seven days*.

c *On the first day* I visited my parents.

d *On that night* there was no moon.

e *In the second year* he decided to go home.

f I could not sleep *for four nights*.

g The emperor kept the consuls waiting *for five hours*.

h Come to see me *at the third hour*.

2 Translate the following sentences:

a Britannī, īrā incēnsī, Rōmānīs fortiter restitērunt.

b puer, gladiīs mīlitum occīsus, ante casam iacēbat.

c mīlitēs fēminās metū commōtās in ōrdinem īnstrūxērunt.

d nōnnūllī prīncipēs, spē praemiī adductī, Salvium adiuvāre cōnstituērunt.

e Salvius Belimicum epistulā dēceptum et nihil suspicātum benignē excēpit.

f Britannī, morte Belimicī monitī, numquam posteā contrā Salvium coniūrāre temptāvērunt.

In each sentence pick out the Latin noun in the ablative case and highlight or underline your translation of it.

Check

Revision

Uses of the cases p. 160

Now that you have met all the cases, this is a good time to check that you know their uses.

1 Cover up the English in italic type on the right. Now see if you can translate the Latin examples on the left.

2 Translate the examples in paragraph 7. Write down the cases of the following nouns and pronouns in the sentences you have just translated.

   a prūdentiae

   b annōs

   c mihi

   d vīnī

   e nōmina iuvenum

   f morte

   g hōrā

   h verbīs Salviī

 Check

Uses of the subjunctive p. 164

Paras 4–6 Read and translate the further examples.

Para. 7 Translate the examples and after each sentence write down the reason why the subjunctive is used, i.e. state what kind of clause it is in. This exercise includes subjunctive clauses that are described on p. 163, so you may need to refer to that page as well.

 Check

General vocabulary practice

Here are some of the words you have met in the Course so far. See if you can do the following exercises without consulting the **Vocabulary**.

1 Which is the odd one out? Give your reason.

a caput	comes	manus	pēs	lingua
b Diana	Iūnō	Mārs	Venus	Minerva
c lēgātus	tribūnus	optiō	prīnceps	centuriō
d haruspex	medicus	nāvis	mercātor	nauta
e probus	sapiēns	scelestus	fortis	vērus
f dīcere	clāmāre	tacēre	poscere	cantāre
g numquam	nox	nūllus	nēmō	nihil
h hōra	nōmen	annus	mēnsis	diēs
i novem	quattuor	vīgintī	mīlle	sexāgintā
j ego	tuus	nōs	tū	vōs

2 Words of opposite meaning. By placing the correct letters in the middle column, match the words on the left with their opposites on the right. The first one is done for you.

	Word	Letter	Opposite word
a	benignus		perfidus
b	ingressus		mors
c	velle	a	crūdēlis
d	mortuus		inimīcus
e	fidēlis		paucī
f	vīta		taceō
g	amīcus		ēgressus
h	clāmō		nōlle
i	aperiō		dēleō
j	aedificō		vīvus
k	terra		mare
l	multī		claudō

3 Arrange the words in each row in order of magnitude, starting with the smallest.

a	urbs	domus	oppidum
b	puer	īnfāns	vir
c	equus	canis	arānea
d	nōnāgintā	quadrāgintā	septuāgintā
e	maximus	maior	magnus
f	mēnsis	annus	diēs
g	mīles	legiō	cohors
h	pugiō	hasta	gladius
i	oculus	dēns	genū
j	flūmen	fōns	mare

Check

Progress record Textbook pp. 121–42   Student Study Book pp. 92–106

Stage 28 imperium	Done	Revised	Any problems?
Model sentences			
testāmentum			
in aulā Salviī			
About the language 1: the ablative case			
cēna Salviī			
About the language 2: expressions of time			
Belimicus rēx			
About the language 3: prepositions			
Interpreting the evidence: Literary evidence			
Archaeological evidence			
Word patterns: adjectives and nouns			
Practising the language			
Interpreting the evidence continued: Inscriptional evidence			
Vocabulary checklist 28			
Language test			
Revision			
General vocabulary practice			

Short guide to the pronunciation of Latin

Short vowels

a   as in English 'aha'

e   as in English 'pet'

i   as in English 'dip'

o   as in English 'pot'

u   as in English 'put'

y   as in French 'plume'

Long vowels (marked as follows)

ā   as in English 'father'

ē   as in French 'fiancée'

ī   as in English 'deep'

ō   as in French 'beau' (roughly as in English 'coat')

ū   as in English 'fool' (not as in 'music')

Diphthongs (two vowels sounded together in a single syllable)

ae   as in English 'high'

au   as in English 'how'

ei   as in English 'day'

eu   no exact English equivalent: 'e' is combined with 'oo' (not as in 'few')

oe   as in English 'boy'

ui   no exact English equivalent: 'u' is combined with 'i'

Consonants

b   (usually) as in English 'big'

b   (followed by t or s) as in English 'lips'

c   as in English 'cat' or 'king' (not as in 'centre' or 'cello')

ch   as in English 'cat' pronounced with emphasis (not as in 'chin')

g   as in English 'got' (not as in 'gentle')

gn   as 'ngn' in English 'hangnail'

i   (before a vowel and sometimes written as j) as in English 'you'

n   (usually) as in English 'net'

n   (before c, g or qu) as in English 'anger'

ph   as in English 'pig' pronounced with emphasis (not as in 'photo')

qu   as in English 'quick'

r   as Scottish ('rolled') r in 'bird'

s   as in English 'sing' (not as in 'roses')

th   as in English 'terrible' pronounced with emphasis (not as in 'the' or 'theatre')

v   (often written as u) as in English 'wind'

x   as in English 'box'

Other consonants are pronounced as in English.

Double consonants

ll   as in English 'hall-light' (not as in 'taller')

nn   as in English 'thin-nosed' (not as in 'dinner')

pp   as in English 'hip-pocket' (not as in 'happy')

Word stress (indicated in this section by *italic type*)

In spoken Latin a syllable in each word is stressed. The following are the general rules for deciding where the stress should fall:

1   In a word of two syllables, the stress is on the first syllable, e.g. *mā*ter, *co*quus.

2   In a word of more than two syllables,

   a)   the stress falls on the second syllable from the end if that syllable contains a long vowel, or a short vowel followed by two consonants, e.g. sa*lū*tat, Me*te*lla;

   b)   otherwise the stress falls on the third syllable from the end, e.g. Cae*ci*lius, *fur*cifer, laet*i*ssimus.

Further examples (with stress marked)

am*ī*cus	*se*det	*vī*lla
*pā*vō	*lae*tus	*lau*dat
*quo*que	la*bō*rat	*ma*gnus
i*ā*nua	*ē*heu	*vī*num
*ver*berat	*quae*rit	*ū*nus